CRYSTALS
FOR BEGINNERS

The Ultimate and Unique Manual for Learning How To Use Gemstone in Manifesting Ritual And Healing Fast

clarifying purposes only and are owned by the owners themselves, not affiliated with this document.

TABLE OF CONTENTS

INTRODUCTION

We will first start with Ancient Egypt. The Crystal Scarab Beetle was used to represent fertility and stability. When the sun shone on it, it would create intense reflections of light throughout the room. This was thought to be a form of magic by those that revered these beetles as gods and goddesses. Crystal also played an important role in their religious ceremonies because they believed that the flesh must be purified before any physical contact is made with the gods and goddesses.

The Egyptians believed that the soul of an animal had to be purified before it could be associated with the gods and goddesses. This was done through the use, or usage, of a crystal ball. The Egyptians also used plate glass and mirrors in their ceremonies as well (Kirchhoff 2nd). They believed that they were doing this in order to gain the power of a god, goddess or spirit animal.

In various religions throughout the ancient world crystals were used to appease or gain favor with spiritual entities. These include...

Ancient Greece- Crystal Balls: The Greeks used balls of clear quartz crystals to represent divinity and power. They also used these balls to seek out possible future events.

The Celts- Crystal Balls: The Celtic culture would use crystal balls in order to look into the future, as well as help them through eternity in their journey to the land of the afterlife.

The Egyptians- Crystal Balls: The ancient Egyptians used crystal balls as a form of divination and also to create beauty.

In order for people, or cultures, from different societies and time periods to interconnect with spiritual entities they needed a medium that was capable of translating the spiritual entities thoughts and feelings. This is where crystals came into play, at least for our purposes here today.

Scarabs would represent the gods, and they could be placed in a ritually dead animal. In this way, the soul of an animal would be translated to the soul of a god. Crystal balls would serve as a mediator for this translation. They could also be used in a variety of religious ceremonies, including sun worship (Ravenscroft 7).

The Crystal Scarab: In Ancient Egypt the scarab beetle was not only revered as divine, it was also considered sacred. The Egyptians referred to it as being alive because it possessed both a physical body and a non-physical soul. This led them to believe that when placed within another living being they could obtain the attributes of their deity. The scarab was considered sacred because the Egyptians believed that they were living reflections of the god Osiris. Thus, when Osiris was murdered by Seth, he was reincarnated within a scarab.

The Egyptians interpreted their relationship with the scarab as one of eternal life. This led them to develop a spiritual or religious ceremony in which they would place the scarab beetle in a mummified body and thus gain powers from their god (Kirchhoff 2nd).

The Egyptians used crystal balls in various ways to help them gain power over death. They would use these to communicate with other gods and goddesses, as well as to purify themselves by contacting their lord and savior Osiris (Ravenscroft 7).

In Ancient Egypt, it was believed that crystal would be able to create a bridge between this world and the afterlife. This is because they believed that a malachite coated beetle would serve as a representation of their lord Osiris. In order for them to follow in his footsteps, they needed to follow the path that he did by following an afterlife similar to the one he followed upon his death. Malachite was chosen because it represented rebirth and immortality (Kirchhoff 3rd).

The Egyptians believed that their god Ra communicated with them through crystals. This is because they knew that crystal could be used as a form of divination and they wanted to know what might happen in the future.

In Ancient Egypt, crystal was used in various magical ceremonies. For instance, they believed that by burning crystals they could meditate upon the afterlife and gain the powers of a god (Kirchhoff 5). They also believed that crystals were to be filled with water, dirt or earth after being burnt in order to serve as a symbol of the underworld (Ravenscroft 7).

The Egyptians also used crystal in order to do something that other cultures have used for centuries: to create beauty.

The use of crystal was becoming more and more important to the Egyptians as time progressed. They began using crystal in their buildings and temples because they thought that this would increase their connection with their god Ra. In order for this to occur, they needed to use the most perfect form of stone they could find. They therefore sought out quartz to make this possible (Ravenscroft 6). Their belief in the spiritual abilities granted to them by crystal was so strong that they began using it in their religious ceremonies as a form of divination. They would often ask questions related to things that were about to or happening presently (Kirchhoff 2nd).

All cultures throughout history have looked at crystals as something more than just a pretty stone. They are used for entertainment, ceremony and meditation. It is my belief that this will never change. No matter how advanced society gets, we will always look to crystals for spiritual guidance.

The earliest use of crystals was for divination in the form of geomancy, which is seeking out answers to questions by interpreting patterns in the earth. These stone diviners would make markings on the ground and interpret what shapes they made that led to answers. This practice dates back nearly 6,000 years ago and it continues today as a popular part of eastern beliefs.

Another use for crystals that dates back thousands of years is to see into other worlds in order to gain knowledge through spiritual journeys. The ancient Greeks and Egyptians both used this practice as a means of wisdom sharing, letting elders teach younger generations through visions with their favorite crystal ball or mirror. These practices lasted long into the Middle Ages when the use of crystals as a tool to seek out answers was almost forgotten.

It wasn't until modern times that crystal healing became popular in western culture as a treatment for everyday ailments from fevers to broken bones. It had it uses, but did not gain widespread popularity until World War II when little else worked for soldiers with serious injuries who were suffering from illnesses that drugs couldn't cure. As a result of modern medicine's focus on chemicals, many natural alternatives for treating disease did not survive the testing process. Crystal healing was among those that did and is still used today to treat various diseases like cancer and arthritis.

There are many ways that crystal healing can be used. Crystals can be worn as jewelry to provide comfort and energy to the wearer. Crystals can also be placed over a part of the body where it will be drawn into the body's energy system to help heal or relieve pain in that area. To relieve pain, a crystal healer might recommend carrying a piece of rock with you or wearing one on a necklace to provide comfort to an injury and prevent further damage.

Ancient Egyptians used crystals on mummies for protection and placed them on tombs as offerings for their dead kings. They were known as "the tears of Isis" and were thought to shine brightly in their afterlife.

Today, crystal healing has become a popular type of alternative medicine. People use precious and semi-precious gemstones in jewelry to promote health. Many people believe that crystals have healing powers and some even claim that certain rocks can protect against evil spirits.

In ancient Greece and Rome, the word 'crystal' was used to describe clear quartz or rock crystal (clear quartz) which was used for scrying as it was believed that visions could be seen through them. In ancient Greece, they also associated quartz with the God of Light Pallas Athena (It is still said that she and her Aegis shield was made from rock crystal).

One of the earliest known uses of quartz crystals was the scrying mirror of Tezcatlipoca, an Aztec god. The Aztecs saw Tezcatlipoca as a powerful deity who ruled over the sun and moon and required that all his followers carry a speculum or small hand-mirror with them at all times.

In Siberia, the Koryak people wore quartz crystals around their necks as protection against evil spirits. In Europe, during the Middle Ages, people believed that crystals were formed from frozen snow and ice and that they contained the power to heal ills. The Florentine Codex (c. 1580) explains how the Aztecs used quartz crystals to foretell the future and cure illnesses. By gazing at their own reflections in a scrying mirror, they hoped to receive answers to their questions and even discover lost objects. The Aztecs would hold the object against their breast and breathe upon it, before asking, "What will happen?"

The ancient records of the Kogi people of present-day Columbia refer to quartz as "the sacred cry of Mother Earth." To them, she spoke through crystals with a message for all humanity: "Honor your mother; protect my children; conserve my resources."

Ancient Europeans also viewed gems as sacred objects that provided protection from evil spirits. In Christian Europe, the belief that gems could ward off the evil eye or bring good luck was widely spread. In fact, in the 13th century, a boy playing with a spherical stone was accused of practicing witchcraft and burned at the stake.

In medieval times, many documents claimed that diamonds had been formed from frozen light at the birth of Christ and were kept inside of a giant crystal by Mary Magdalene. One legend holds that diamonds were formed when sunlight hit water containing plentiful diamonds. The crystals then rose to the surface of the water and melted together as they reached equilibrium temperature.

Because of their amazing properties and beauty, it was only a matter of time before the stones were gifted to royalty. The first documented use of diamonds in Europe was by the Hungarian king St. Stephen I who was wearing an amethyst ring in 1046. By the 12th century, diamonds were a standard gift for European monarchs and the nobility. Indeed, these stones were so valuable that a legend grew up that diamond cuts could not be stolen. However, in 1759, King Louis XV of France had his diamond collection stolen by jewelers Francois Balsan (France) and Claude Gand (Italy).

Jacob von Uffenbach in 1790 presented some of these diamond cut stones to the world at the Berlin exhibition. Diamonds were eventually reserved for royalty, though gem traders could often acquire a large number of them at no cost. On average, it was said that a stone valued at 10,000 gulden was priced at only 100 gulden. However, while diamonds were considered valuable and valuable enough to be stolen by jewelers, it was not long before they became regarded as highly addictive and the dealers profiting from the practice were known as 'diamond cutters'.

It was not until 1846 that the first recorded diamond hoax occurred in Europe. This was as a result of the French Revolution. A pair of diamond-studded spurs were made for Louis Napoleon Bonaparte, then President of the Second Republic. The pair were meant to be sent to him by his brother Emperor Napoleon III. In fact, they were made of paste and it was thought that they would be better suited for a goose call!

For almost 200 years, diamonds remained one of the most highly valued and sought after stones in the world, especially in Europe. In 1877, they became a symbol of wealth and luxury during Queen Victoria's Diamond Jubilee Celebration. They were often seen with gemstones like rubies, emeralds and sapphires as a combination of precious stones were also sometimes known as 'diamonds'.

However, diamonds were always associated with the idea of eternal love. In 1882, The Great Exhibition showcased an impressive display of black diamonds from South Africa. Though the stones originally came from India, they were meant to be acquired by European traders using slaves.

From the 15th to 19th centuries, diamond mining in South America was common. At first it was mostly from the colony of New Spain (Mexico), but by the mid-16th century it had spread to Peru and Brazil. After this point, the mines in all three countries became increasingly known as 'El Dorado', which means the place of gold. The name was applied to a lost city of wealth and prosperity beyond the imagination. In reality, only small amounts of precious stones were actually found in South America, but they were generally more valuable than those found elsewhere. As diamonds became more widely traded, it was almost impossible to not have heard of them.

The first great diamond rush occurred when the Egyptians began to import diamonds from India in 1837. This was the start of a series of rushes that continued until most production had been moved from India to other areas. At the time, South Africa and Brazil were the traditional sources of diamonds.

In 1869, De Beers succeeded in embedding diamonds in a matrix of cement so that they could be easily cut and polished. The method used became known as the ear-diamond or champagne diamond when it was first used at the court of Queen Mary II. This method was soon adopted by others with De Beers retaining a monopoly on sales for many years. However, new methods were being invented all the time and by 1880, there had been an explosion in production due to new methods for cutting and polishing which were now being used around South Africa.

In 1913, the tumbling mill was invented. This sped up the cutting process by a great deal and was used to cut diamonds which had not yet been embedded in cement. The need for these stones increased all over the world after World War I, making South Africa the leading producer of diamonds in the world. Once war broke out again, South Africa had to produce a huge number of gold and diamond rings for soldiers, with production reaching 300 000 per week by 1945.

South African mines were nationalized in 1954 and amalgamated into De Beers Consolidated Mines Ltd (DBCM). The Kerr-McGee Corporation, an American mining company, purchased DBCM in 1987. This merger was the first of its kind in the history of transnational corporations. Now known as De Beers Consolidated Mines (DBCM), this company has since overseen five major mergers with other South African mining companies.

In 1983, DBCM began consolidating all its diamond mines into a single company: De Beers Consolidated Mines Limited (DBCML). The company's private equity investors eventually lost patience with the continued underperformance and its privatization was announced in January 2006. The company was then listed on the London Stock Exchange in May 2007.

During World War II, the US War Department conducted research into an alternative way to cut diamonds. Joseph P. Kennedy started to manufacture diamonds and created a method by which they could be manufactured in large quantities for industrial use. In addition, he also developed new applications for them such as lasers, electrical switches and even synthetic gemstones. Due to wartime restrictions, however, very little of his work was made available until after the war's end.

After World War II, the market became flooded with diamonds. De Beers in South Africa and Anglo American in South America were the two major producers of diamond in the world. By 1949, the end of World War II had seen an influx of diamonds coming into France and Germany as a result of reparations to Britain and France. Within ten years, it was considered that their reparation payments would not be fully paid so they were forced to sell their share of the world's diamond production.

In 1952, De Beers and Tiffany & Co. entered into a partnership. In 1955, De Beers acquired more than 22% of Tiffany & Co. stock to get control of its shares. They then opened the world's first diamond store in New York, United States.

THE HEALING PROPRIETIES OF CRYSTALS

For a long time, crystals have been an important part of human life. They are used in many different circumstances and for many different purposes. Nowadays, people use them to feel better and heal themselves from any number of problems that they're experiencing. If you want to know more about how crystal healing can help you, this will be your guide.

We all experience difficulties in our lives – some more than others! When the going gets tough, it can sometimes seem like there is no way out and hope is lost; however, at those moments we need something to believe in the most.

Crystals enhance or boost your own energy to get you through the hard times and to help you solve problems so that you can move forward again.

These stones are energetic in nature, and they can be used for healing purposes. They are considered to be some of the best things that we can use for our health and happiness. Here at crystalwarehouse.co.uk we have a wide selection of crystals that you can buy; these are all available in our online shop.

Crystals and their Healing Properties

There are many different kinds of crystals, each with their own healing properties. Some of the best known to us include:

Amethyst – this beautiful purple stone is a very common variety, and it has been used for centuries as a natural remedy. It is very helpful if someone is experiencing or recovering from drug abuse or addiction. It also helps if they are dealing with any kind of stress or anxiety. Amethyst is great for relaxation, and it also helps you to get rid of negative emotions such as anger, fear, and even jealousy. The color of the stone is said to bring happiness and success to many people, and it can also improve your overall health. It is a powerful crystal that works out of any situation and enhances all of your abilities. This stone tends to be recommended for those who love purple things, or those who are single and in need of romance.

Clear quartz – this kind of crystal has been used for a very long time in ancient times. It is one of the most powerful healing crystals on this planet. It can heal nearly anything that you may have; it can even help with problems with the heart or the mind. This stone is known to bring happiness, courage, and a positive attitude to those who use it. It is also a good choice if you are going through any intense or difficult times – it works wonders for you! You can use this stone to help heal the mind, body, and spirit.

Rose quartz – this kind of crystal has an excellent reputation for being able to protect its owner from illness or even death. The power of rose quartz is said to be very great and sacred on a spiritual level as well as on an emotional level. It's an excellent healing crystal that helps you in many different ways, and it is very powerful when dealing with problems relating to your heart. It is one of the best-known types of crystals in the world.

Calcite – this kind of crystal is one of the oldest ones on our planet. It works like many other crystals, and it can help you deal with many different kinds of issues such as heart pain, disease, and a lot more. This kind of stone has been used all over the world for a very long time when it comes to healing purposes; it's known to be very effective even today. It's amazing what many people have already achieved using this crystal! This mineral is very calming and soothing; it can even help with anxiety if you are feeling anxious in any way. It is known to bring happiness and good luck to those who use it.

Sodalite – this is another crystal that has been used for many years, and it is also very helpful when dealing with problems relating to the mind or the emotions. It promotes peace of mind, and it can also heal you if you have any problems with your heart or your feelings. It's a very good stone to have in your life! It makes you happy and relaxed, and it helps you deal with difficult situations that may be making your life difficult. This crystal is recommended for those who are looking for ease and comfort.

Lapis Lazuli – this type of crystal is another one that has been used all over the world as long as humans have existed on our planet. Today, it's a very popular stone that can help you in many different ways. If you are healing something physical, it can help. If you are healing something mental or emotional, it works just as well. This stone promotes patience and fairness, and it helps you to overcome all kinds of difficult situations and problems. This type of crystal has been used for centuries for many different purposes!

Many more kinds of crystals exist on our planet today, each with their own specific purposes and healing properties. You don't have to be sick or injured to use these kinds of stones. They can work for you in any situation. They can even help you deal with your own problems and emotions if you happen to be feeling bad in any way – this is a very good thing!

If you are like me, you may be looking for ways to help with your insomnia. You might toss and turn through the night, wondering why the best sleeping aids that doctors prescribe do not seem to have the same effects. You may even resort to drinking coffee, which has become your primary caffeine source throughout the day- despite having a tolerance for this stimulant. In my experience, I find that Crystal Quartz is one of the most effective healing techniques I have at my disposal when it comes time to find some restful sleep. I would like to explore the healing powers of Crystal Quartz.

The Healing Properties of Quartz Crystals

These beautiful minerals are here to teach us about consciousness and the power of our thoughts. They can help heal physical ailments as well as spiritual ones. Given that it is one of the most powerful healing crystals, it is important for you to learn how it can help you find restful sleep at night.

Quartz Crystals have been used for healing since ancient times. The Ancient Greeks believed it to be a gift from the gods. The word "quartz" comes from the German word "quartz" which means "hard rock". In modern times, quartz crystals are now used by healers throughout the world. Crystal Quartz is thought to help with the following ailments: chronic fatigue syndrome, bowel disorders, muscular pain and cramps, influenza and other viral infections including AIDS, insomnia and restlessness. These are only a few of the ailments that Quartz will reportedly clear up. Given that it is a powerful healing crystal, it should come as no surprise that Crystal Quartz can help you get some restful sleep at night.

How Do Crystal Quartz Crystals Work?

The combination of the various chemicals contained within each crystal can produce different effects. In general, the chemicals that make up Quartz crystals can help to cleanse the body and mind. Since it is believed to help with so many ailments, it should come as no surprise what Crystal Quartz does for your health. Sometimes, you may find that you are back in bed at 2am unable to sleep because a certain thought keeps running through your head which makes you anxious. You try to go back to bed, but find yourself sitting upright staring at the ceiling all night long. This is because your mind can be mentally wired with all kinds of fears and concerns. If you find yourself in this situation, you should try a crystal that helps to cleanse the mind. Given that it has been used for thousands of years, I would recommend using Quartz to aid your sleep.

Why Crystal Quartz Crystals Can Help You Sleep

As part of the process of clearing the mind, it helps to use a crystal that is able to absorb negative energy from the body. The crystals that are able to cleanse negative energies are vastly beneficial for people who struggle with restful sleep at night. Given that many of us are out in the world being exposed to a lot of negative energy throughout the day, it should come as no surprise to learn that emotional stress is one of the most common causes of insomnia. If you find yourself in a situation where your mind is overloaded with all kinds of thoughts, it can be difficult to sleep.

There is no doubt that in this day and age, we are living in a fast paced world. Though we like to believe that our modern conveniences make our life easier, it is actually changing the way we live for the worse. We have seen how technology has made it difficult for us to unplug and connect with each other as human beings. Mobile phones keep us connected even when we are sitting right next to each other and video games are making it hard for children to be imaginative as they play instead of watching TV or playing outside. To counter all of these negatives, many people turn to crystals as a means of detoxification through spiritual cleansing, which also brings about healing.

Crystals are a great way to eliminate your daily stress and allow you to take a step back from the world to center yourself and heal. When it comes to healing, there are numerous different methods that can be used. However you choose to heal, crystals can help you on your journey. One of the best ways for you to use crystals for healing is by using a crystal syphon. In order to use this process, all you have to do is fill one end of the glass bottle with water and place any kind of crystal that makes sense for your healing into the bottle. Then, close the bottle as tight as possible and let it sit overnight as you go about your normal daily activities. In the morning, you will see that the water has changed color and there are particles collected in the bottle. Pour out the old water and rinse the bottle to clear it out, then refill it with fresh water and place a new crystal inside. You can also make use of a crystal syphon to choose a gemstone for your zodiac sign or for different parts of your body which need healing.

It is important to note that crystals are powerful tools when used correctly yet they can be harmful if not handled correctly. One of the most common causes of harm to this process is people putting too much water into the bottle. Water can be replaced but it can be difficult to recreate the same healing environment that you once had, so do not risk harming your crystal syphon by overdoing it. Some of the more experienced users of this process have found out that there are some crystals that cannot be healed with a crystal syphon and some stones will react differently when used in this manner while others simply do not respond when placed in a syrup or a water syphon. Before purchasing these items, be sure you know what you are buying and let them help you find out if your stone is compatible with this method of healing.

One of the best ways that you can benefit from these techniques is to create a list of your problems and symptoms. When you have listed all of these items, you can then choose a crystal that will resonate with each one to help you solve these issues, as well as to help keep them at bay so that they do not become worse.

After performing a crystal syphon, the most important thing is to maintain your connection with the crystal. You should perform this process once every two weeks in order for it to properly cleanse your body and mind. Be sure not to re-use the same crystal more than three times at one time since this could begin affecting its energy and healing properties rather than enhancing them. It is ideal to switch out your crystal every time you perform this process in order to keep your mind, body and spirit well balanced and resistant to harm.

Crystal healing is all about unconditional love and acceptance that helps people release their barriers and begin a new way of living that's more fulfilling. Plus, it helps you recognize your true self in order to facilitate personal growth. Crystal therapy can also help alleviate anxiety or depression, improve self-confidence, and raise energy levels so that people can finally live up to their full potential.

Crystal Therapy is the practice of harnessing the healing power of crystals to promote physical, emotional, and spiritual well-being. It is also known as crystal healing or crystal medicine. Crystal therapy works on a principle similar to acupressure, where the energy fields of the body are manipulated with the use of crystals. Crystals can be used in a number of ways:

Crystal therapy is based on a belief that each individual possesses an energy field around him, called aura. This aura holds one's individual life force or chi (also known as prana). All events, experiences, and emotions in one's life affect the aura. These energetic imprints play a crucial role in one's health and well-being.

Crystal therapy helps to clear these imprints from the aura. To do this, certain crystals are placed on various points of the body corresponding to different aspects of an individual's life (physical problems, mental or emotional well-being, etc.). Crystals have different vibrations depending upon their chemical composition. These vibrations help restore balance to the flow of energy within an individual through the energy field around him. This reintegrated energy flow improves health and helps foster a sense of inner harmony or peace.

Crystal therapy can be used to help resolve issues such as anger, addiction, anxiety, arthritis, asthma, backache, burnout, cancer, chronic fatigue syndrome/fibromyalgia, colds/flu/sinusitis/ear problems/ear infections (children), depression and emotional trauma (including post-traumatic stress disorder), diabetes and other blood sugar imbalances (including hypoglycemia), ear problems (ears ringing), eczema or dry skin conditions (acne also may respond to stone healing), emotional trauma and PTSD, eyestrain issues and other vision problems (like nearsightedness or astigmatism), fatigue and feeling tired all the time. It can help to improve overall energy and reduce stress.

It is strongly recommended that individuals who are interested in crystal therapy consult with a trained practitioner before undertaking any large-scale work. As stated above, crystal healing works well with the high vibration of our chakras – allowing us to receive more of what we truly desire. If you are new to the process of self-healing, it may take a couple of sessions before you see major results, as crystals work best in pairs (or better yet, groups).

Like herbal medicine, crystal healing also has its own unique set of side effects; which means nothing is "negative" with regards to these therapies. More often than not, these include fatigue, insomnia, dizziness and headaches. Although minor issues such as these eventually subside, it is important not to get discouraged when experiencing any type of side effects while undergoing healing.

The goal of crystal therapy is to work with the patient's energy fields in order to achieve inner peace and balance. As crystal healing progresses, one must also learn how to recognize which crystals are appropriate for which purpose. You should be able to combine the right crystals with their corresponding hand positions in a way that will resonate within your own energy field. Crystals can also work together to help create healing synergy, as their energies will complement one another.

HOW MANIFESTATION WORKS

There's nothing new about the concept of using the power of your mind to create reality.

Napoleon Hill was writing about manifestation as far back as 1937 – you may have heard of his famous book, Think and Grow Rich.

But there's plenty of evidence that civilizations knew about the power of the human mind to create reality for many generations before that. The difference is that in the past this knowledge was always kept secret by shamans, medicine men, wise women, priests and witch doctors.

No wonder, when you think about it, because manifestation has the power to change lives beyond recognition. And it's right that nowadays this information is available to each and every one of us. Of course, in the past, "experts" in creating reality – what we would now call manifestation – didn't really know how it works, and they tended to end up attributing the appearance of what they wanted in their lives either to prayer or to the intervention of God. Nowadays we know a lot more about how the universe works, so we can make some suggestions about the nature of manifestation.

atomic science has shown us that all matter is simply energy.

It's a paradox that things which appear solid are, when you get down to the atomic level, just a form of pure energy. That's because atoms can take the form of solid particles or energy. And it's the interchange of energy and matter which could be at the root of our ability to manifest things in our world.

The term manifestation simply means to create reality or to bring something into being.

People talk about manifestation in different ways, but what it really means is the act of creating or acquiring things, or changing the world around you, with the power of your mind.

So you might want to manifest physical objects like a new car or a new house. You might want to manifest greater prosperity or better health, or abundant joy. Or perhaps you want to manifest a loving relationship or some great vision you have....

A lot of people like to talk about the concept of "co-creation". This recognizes the fact that you don't manifest anything alone. Somehow, somewhere, the universe is involved in co-creating your reality with you. For religious nature, the universe probably means God. Cocreation probably means prayer. For other people, the universe can mean things like cosmic consciousness or universal intelligence, or the universal mind or infinite intelligence. Other people talk about The Great Mystery or The Oneness. In a way it doesn't matter what framework of beliefs you put onto manifestation because all of these ideas are fundamentally the same:
they recognize that our minds can communicate with something bigger than ourselves.

In short, we can communicate in some way with the universe beyond our minds and bodies - and by doing so we can impel the universe to change the reality around us.

if everything is known to the universal intelligence – or God – then it follows that if you communicate with it in the right way, asking, let's say, for greater prosperity, then the universal intelligence already knows exactly how to manifest that for you.

USING CRYSTALS FOR YOUR MANIFESTING PRACTICE

Crystals are amazing. Forged in the Earth over thousands - and in some cases millions - of years, crystals are more than just shiny rocks that are pretty to look at. These gems have centuries of the Earth's energy stored within them. But how do we take that energy and use them for manifesting?

Crystals are unique in that they have the ability to help you emotionally, physically and spiritually. Now if that sounds a little too "woo" for you, remember this: crystals have been relied upon and used for centuries to help heal.
Each crystal has a unique vibrational energy that can be used in a variety of ways. From cleansing negative energy from a space, healing old emotional wounds, opening up stagnant energy in your Chakras, fostering feelings of self-love and abundance and even helping you connect with your intuition, crystals have the innate ability to help you really tap into your truest wants, desires and needs.

When added to a manifesting practice, you can harness that vibrational energy and help speed your results.

CLEANSING YOUR CRYSTALS

Before you begin manifesting you will first need cleanse your Crystal, they are energetic and can absorb any negative energy come in contact with. This is why it is important to always cleanse, charge and set an intention for your stone before you begin working with it.
Luckily, this process is not difficult and in fact can be a lot of fun

Here the 3 easy way to Cleanse it:

1. Clean it: wash your crystal under cold running water for few minute or in salt water for an hour for remove the negativity
2. Back to earth: bury for a minimum of 24 hours for returning your crystal to the earth vibration
3. Turn on incense (or sage) : run the stone through the smoke for a complete purification and left the window open for allow the negativity flow back in the atmosphere

CHARGING YOUR CRYSTALS

After cleansing you are going to need to charge your crystals. Charging just means you are putting energy back into the crystal and allowing it to function at it's highest frequency.

Anytime you cleanse a crystal you should charge it. The charging process is simple. You can charge in nature or through visualization.

CHARGING IN NATURE: place your crystal in sunlight or moonlight for 6-12 hours. Always look up your stone first to find out which is appropriate (some crystals like amethyst lose color in the sun).

CHARGING THROUGH VISUALIZATION: hold your crystal in your dominant hand and visualize a white light coming down from the Universe, traveling through the chakras in your body and into the crystal.

INTENTIONS

TO SET YOUR INTENTION: Hold the crystal in your dominant hand and clear your mind of any negative thoughts. Clearly state your intention and your desire. When setting an intention, think of the bigger picture. Say you were using Citrine. You wouldn't say "I want to win the lottery Instead, think of your desired outcome. "I am open to bring new financial opportunities into my life and have the courage to pursue them" would open you up to more possibilities.

Each crystal you choose (or that chooses you) has a vibration and energy that is designed to help you. Tap into the meaning of your stone and choose and intention that will be amplified by the natural energy of the crystal.

Setting intentions is a powerful way to manifest happiness, love and stability in your life. the more powerful the intention, so don't be afraid to speak your intention out loud or write it in your journal

CRYSTALS TO BOOST CREATIVITY

Crystal is a unique substance with a wide range of healing properties. The most commonly known and used crystal, it can improve energy in just about any aspect of your life. Crystal has also been said to promote creativity by enhancing serenity and opening pathways for creative ideas. Here are some crystals to help you find that hidden spark or channel your creativity in an entirely new way!

1. Selenite: This crystal is perfect for helping you keep peace with yourself when things get overly chaotic at work or home. It can help you see clearly even when others are clouding your judgement, which will allow you to see the bigger picture and reach creative solutions more easily.

2. Aventurine: Aventurine will help you channel your positive energy as well as enhance your creativity. Layering this crystal on top of itself will allow you to fully harness its potential to open up new creative avenues for an entirely new level of creative expression.

3. Moonstone: This crystal is an excellent choice for those who have a hard time focusing or improvising on the fly, whether it be in business or art. It is a powerful tool to aid in creating original ideas and even has the potential to stimulate inspiration at will!

4. Tiger's Eye: The tiger's eye is one of the most common crystals used for helping with any type of healing. This crystal aids in releasing restrictions and blocks that are hindering your creativity. It can also help boost your intuition, allowing you to draw on information from many sources when seeing the big picture of a situation.

5. Labradorite: Labradorite is great for those who have been struggling with connecting their creative work with their financial success. It will aid you in understanding how your work can be used to bring about a positive change in the world around you. Use this crystal to help clear old habits and become more efficient at fulfilling any creative potential that you may have locked up inside of yourself!

6. Hematite: Use this crystal to help you become more confident in your own abilities. Hematite breaks down barriers you may have been conditioned to believe prevent you from attaining creative success. As a result, this crystal can help to break down your fears and create an environment that will allow you to let go of the old and start anew!

7. Moldavite: Moldavite is a fantastic choice for those who need a boost in their creativity or desire new avenues for expression. It has been said that moldavite has the ability to channel positive energy into objects it is placed upon. This will allow you to use your creativity in new ways such as healing others or invoking spontaneous ideas in the moment!

8. Iolite: This crystal can help you let go of negativity and stress so that you can better deal with the day to day issues that may be blocking your paths to creativity. Iolite can help you focus your energy on what's most important, empowering you to manifest positive change in your life!

9. Smoky Quartz: Use smoky quartz for those who find themselves losing sight of their goals and needs. This crystal can simply be used as a reminder to pursue your dreams, which will allow you to move through any obstacles on the way!

10. Rose Quartz: Rose quartz is a crystal of love and it also will help to remove old patterns and ideas that may be holding you back from your true creative potential. This crystal can help build up confidence so that you can pursue your own personal goals without fear of failure!

11. Green Aventurine: If you are looking for a creative boost while manifesting a new project or career, this crystal will aid in the manifestation process while also helping to clear any unwanted blockages or negative energy. Green Aventurine is perfect for those who need a boost in their lives by invigorating their passion for life and starting anew!

12. Jade: It is said that jade is a powerful tool for those who are unable to use their right sides of the brain. It will help you break down barriers and activate your creative potential by giving you the ability to freely think outside the box!

13. Apatite: Apatite is one of the most versatile crystals available for helping you harness your creativity potential. It can be used on anything from tools to garments, and even jewelry, to imbue it with creative power!

14. Amber: Amber has a very long history of being used in healing ceremonies and rituals across almost every culture in history. It is a very versatile gift and can even be used to help you harness the power of your own creativity!

15. Howlite: This crystal will help you break down any negative patterns or thoughts that are holding you back from being your most creative self. It can also help to clear energy on a physical level as well!

16. Orange Calcite: Use this crystal when you need an extra boost of creativity before an important meeting or presentation. This crystal will help you to feel confident, protected, and at ease in front of other people, which will allow your natural creative flair to shine through!

17. Herkimer Diamond: This crystal is a powerful tool for strengthening any facet of your life. It will help you to break down barriers and use your creative talents in new ways!

18. Aquamarine: If you are undergoing any type of healing or transformation, this crystal will help you maintain patience with yourself during the process. You can use it to aid you in keeping positive thoughts that will keep you going while working through any issues!

19. Jadeite: This green crystal is a fantastic choice for those who desire money and prosperity on the material plane. It will help to open up new avenues for creativity and success!

20. Amethyst: Amethyst is a fantastic tool for helping you tap into your spiritual creativity. It will give you an inner peace that will help to clear your mind and open you up to new ideas and possibilities!

21. Turquoise: This stone is a wonderful companion for those who need a gentle push in their creative endeavors. It will help you break down barriers while encouraging your own unique creativity to shine through!

22. Rhodochrosite: This crystal will activate the power of compassion, allowing you to feel more empathy towards yourself and others around you. This can help ease the stresses of everyday life and allow your natural beauty to come forth!

23. Black Tourmaline: This crystal will help to activate your creativity, allowing you to flow with the universe while staying grounded at the same time!

24. Labradorite: Labradorite is a wonderful choice for activating your creative energies. It will allow you to break free of any negative thought patterns or old habits that are holding you back from living life fully!

25. Blue Calcite: This stone will give you the energy and confidence that will allow you to live in the world flawlessly, both in your personal and professional lives!

26. Rutile: Use this crystal when navigating through scenarios that test your creativity and spontaneity. It will give you the ability to embrace the spontaneous feelings that will bring your creativity and vibrancy to full bloom!

27. Hematite: This crystal will increase your self-confidence, allowing you to find what it is that you really want in life! You can use this crystal to help build up your inner power so that you can deal with those who would try to bring you down!

28. Apophyllite: This stone is a fantastic choice for those who want emotional healing. It gives off a gentle energy that will help calm the mind and allow thoughts of love and inner peace to flow freely!

29. Black Tourmaline: This crystal will help you to live your life fully and completely without feeling the need to hold anything back!

30. Tiger's Eye: Tiger's Eye is a wonderful crystal if you are experiencing anxiety or depression. It will help to ground you and keep you in the present of what is happening in the moment!

31. Rhodochrosite: This stone will bring soothing vibrations to your body, relieving any stress that may be creating a disturbance in your daily life!

32. Tourmalated Quartz: This crystal is great for people who are always making sure that they are on top of things and planning well enough ahead of time. You can place one of these in your car, in your home, or purse to help you to say "yes" to the ideas that come to you at the most unexpected times!

33. Black Tourmaline: This crystal will help you find some inner peace and bring a sense of tranquility to your life.

34. Sardonyx: Sardonyx is great for people who feel that they have too many responsibilities and are finding it difficult to keep up with everything. This crystal will give you a sense of calm and peace so that you can make a little room for yourself! It is also a very good stone for enhancing psychic abilities!

35. Apatite: Apatite is a wonderful addition to any crystal collection that many people just aren't aware that they need it! This crystal will help you to let go of fears and burdens so that you can truly live life to its fullest potential!

36. Jet: Jet is a very powerful cleanser, as it will clear away any energy that may be holding you back from your true creative potential. It will also aid in raising your vibration to higher levels of creativity.

37. Jasper: Jasper is a wonderful tool for those who want to use their creative powers to help others in need. It will bring great healing and protection to your life so that you can be the most effective possible human being at any given time!

38. Morganite: Morganite is an excellent way to balance your feminine side with your masculine abilities, allowing you to work more effectively towards your goals in life.

39. Sodalite: This stone will enhance your intuition and make it easier for you to work with any type of energies that may be blocking you from reaching your true potential.

40. Sodalite is a wonderful healer on every level of its being. It gives off a very gentle and soothing energy. This energy will prevent any blockages from occurring in your life, and clear away any negative thought patterns that may be keeping you stuck!

41. Black Tourmaline: This incredible crystal will bring you a lot of emotional healing and help to open up your heart chakras so that you can breathe deep into the possibilities of life!

42. Iolite: Use this stone to allow yourself to let go of the stress and worry in your life, so that you can truly shine in all areas of your life!

43. Moldavite: Moldavite is a fantastic addition to any crystal collection! It will help you to activate your creative talents and abilities by opening up new avenues for inspiration!

44. Aquamarine: This stone is incredibly beautiful and will allow you to have wonderful dreams, thoughts, and visions that will allow you to work through any issues that you may be facing in life! It is also great for clearing away old habits of thought that are no longer serving you!

45. Rose Quartz: This stone is a great tool for bringing gentleness into your life. It will help calm the mind and give off a very relaxing energy that will make everything seem possible!

46. Aquamarine: This stone will help to bring clarity and focus into your life, allowing you to live life with a great sense of calm and peace!

47. Turquoise: Turquoise will clear away any old thought patterns and habits that no longer serve you in life! It will help you to activate your creative energies so that you can truly live the life that you have been dreaming of!

48. Jet: Jet can be used for treating various types of skin problems, especially acne. This crystal is also a very powerful cleanser for clearing away any negative energy or clutter from your mind and body!

49. Moonstone: Moonstone is a wonderful crystal to use when you are going through some type of healing process. Use it to help you heal from your past worries and any negativity that has come to you in the present!

50. Calcite: Calcite will help balance out any emotional imbalances in your life. It can be used either externally for pain relief or on an internal level for tissues and bone healing!

51. Black Obsidian: Black Obsidian is a great tool for dealing with emotional issues that may have to come up in your life. It will help you to ignore negative thought patterns and bring about a sense of calm so that you can get rid of any negative energy!

52. Fluorite: This crystal will bring lots of balance to your life. It will allow you to listen well to the world around you, as well as draw you toward many intriguing possibilities for the future!

53. Sodalite: If there are any areas in your life that may be holding you back from reaching your true potential, use Sodalite for emotional healing and cleansing. This crystal will help you to integrate any other crystals that you may have into your life so that they can truly work for you!

54. Lava: Lava is a powerful tool for activating your creative energies and allowing them to flow freely. It will also allow you to embrace the new ideas and inspirations that come into your life!

55. Pink Tourmaline: This stone brings in a lot of energy and light into every area of your life, which can help you live more fully. It will also allow you to open up yourself up to great ideas, thoughts, inspirations, and dreams!

56. Blue Obsidian: This stone brings in a powerful energy that will break any negative thought patterns and outdated habits that you may have! It will help you to move forward with your life, letting go of anything and anyone that is preventing you from living life fully!

57. Topaz: Use Topaz to let go of those past hurts and pains that are causing you to feel depressed or anxious. This crystal also helps to open the spiritual chakras in order for you to understand the true meaning of love!

58. Rose Quartz: Rose Quartz is a fantastic crystal for those who have difficulties accepting love in their life. It will help you to open up your heart so that you can truly live a life with love and happiness!

59. Serpentine: This stone brings in all of your creative energies and helps you to direct them in a positive way! You can use this stone to keep any negative thoughts from ever entering your mind ever again!

60. Blue Chalcedony: This crystal is great for people who want to reach for the stars and take that leap into the next phase of their lives. It is a wonderful stone for activating your creativity, allowing you to make use of your unique talents and abilities in the world around you!

61. Bloodstone: This crystal is a wonderful way to release any negative emotions from your life. It will also help you to see the possibilities that lie within yourself, as well as in others!

62. Serpentine: This stone will help you to release all of the stress that has been holding you back from living the life that you want. It will allow you to feel comfortable in your own skin, and even share with others who need a little more love and kindness in their lives!

63. Andalusite: Andalusite is a powerful healer, as it will help you to move forward in your life with ease. It will bring your emotions into harmony with your thoughts and ideas, allowing you to move forward into the wonderful world of tomorrow!

64. Alien Aura Quartz: This crystal has a very soothing energy that will allow you to open up all of the chakras in your body and release yourself from any energy blocks that may have been interfering with this process!

65. Rose Quartz: This crystal is a very powerful healer that will help you to release all of the love and affection that you may have been holding back! It can also release any negative feelings of fear and allow you to embrace the future with great possibilities!

CRYSTALS TO HELP EASE ANXIETY AND DEPRESSIVE THOUGHT

If you, or someone you know, are dealing with anxiety or depressive thought circuits, then the best option would be to incorporate these crystals into your daily life. All of them can be used as both a physical and mental tool to help heal those who are battling these thoughts.

In this we'll talk about what each crystal does, the emotional state they're great for handling or healing, and how one might use them in their daily life.

So without further ado:

Crystal 1 - Variscite: Works well for anxiety and depressive thought circuits that stem from being worried about other people's opinions of oneself. It can also balance out mood by keeping one uplifted in difficult situations.

Crystal 2 - Auralite: Works wonderfully to heal depression and anxiety that stem from other people's opinions about oneself, especially those who have no control over what others think of them. It's also great for anxiety and depressive thought circuits that are inexplicable and often difficult to explain.

Crystal 3 - Hyophorite: Considering how deeply connected we all are, it's no wonder this crystal can be used for depression and anxiety that stem from losing individual identity in the group (i.e., one doesn't feel like they fit in anymore with others). It can also balance out mood by keeping one uplifted in difficult situations.

Crystal 4 - Lepidolite: Can be used for depression and anxiety that stem from thinking that others have more power or influence than they really do.

Crystal 5 - Illite: Works wonderfully to heal depression and anxiety that stem from not feeling like the person you are in reality matches up to the person you'd like yourself to be.

Crystal 6 - Natrolite: Works wonderfully to heal depression and anxiety that stem from thoughts about other people's negative opinions of oneself, especially if they relating to "baggage" from the past with regards to relationships.

Crystal 7 - Kunzite: This gem has a wide range of uses, but its magical properties can easily be assigned to heal depression and anxiety that stem from thinking others will never like the person one really is.

Crystal 8 - Siderite: Works wonderfully to heal depression and anxiety that stem from other people's opinions about oneself, especially those who have no control over what others think of them.

Crystal 9 - Natrolite: Works wonderfully to heal depression and anxiety that stem from not feeling like the person you are in reality matches up to the person you'd like yourself to be.

Ben Franklin once stated "An ounce of prevention is worth a pound of cure". It's a simple statement but one that is true in almost any situation.

Nurture Your Mind, Heal Your Body

The central theme of this website is that our emotional state can have a profound effect on our physical condition. We are what we think. Our feelings create our reality. If we feel sick then we're more likely to get sick.

So the most important thing for us to do with regards to physical health is nurture the mind, so that healthy emotional habits can be developed on a regular basis. This will create a strong foundation for physical healing.

I will talk about 3 different stones which help soothe the mind and balance out mood by keeping us uplifted in difficult situations. We'll cover each one's individual properties, including the emotional state it helps with and why this state of mind is important for overall physical health.

Meditating on Emotional State

Meditation is an ancient relaxation technique that's been around for thousands of years. Although it's often looked upon as something of a religion or a spiritual practice, it can actually be used to restore balance to our mental health and mind-body connection.

Ideally, one should meditate on a daily basis. (If you have never done it before, you may want to practice 4 times a week at first). The times to meditate are in the morning and at night before bed.

The best way to meditate is sitting in lotus position while looking into a crystal. You can also sit up straight while looking at an object that represents your spiritual beliefs (i.e., church iconography, religious painting, etc.).

Inhale deeply through your nose and exhale through your mouth. Always start your meditations with a few minutes of breathing exercises.

The point of meditation is to clear the mind, promote relaxation, and reestablish balance in the body.

Here are four steps to follow:

1.) Breathe in deeply for 5 seconds.

2.) Breathe out slowly for 10 seconds.

3.) Inhale deeply while counting to 9 (the ending number is up to you). This allows time for negative thoughts or emotions (i.e., anger, frustration, or fear) to fully leave the body through exhalation. 4.) Exhale slowly while counting from 1-8 and then finish by taking one more deep breath as you count from 1-20. (a) Repeat this for 5-15 minutes (b) Take a short break while repeating steps 3 & 4 for 5-10 minutes. Then finish with a final condensed version of step 4 that lasts from 1-20.

The number of breaths you take is totally up to you. You may also choose to perform the breathing portions as often as you wish throughout your meditation.

For most people, the best time for meditation is in the morning, but if you find it difficult to wake up early then do it at night before going to sleep.

Crystal 1 - Amethyst: This crystal has long been used in meditation and relaxation exercises because of its power to soothe overworked minds and relieve stress and anxiety.

Amethyst is the master healer of the mind and emotions. It's a stone that instills peace, tranquility, and mental stability. It can be used to treat insomnia, depression, anxiety, stress, fatigue, and common mood disorders.

The most ideal time for meditation with Amethyst is in the morning.

Some suggested visualization techniques to improve emotional well-being with Amethyst are: (a) Holding it during moments of emotional distress (i.e., family troubles). However if you suffer from an autoimmune condition like Lupus or Scleroderma then avoid holding Amethyst since it has an aggravating effect on some autoimmune symptoms if held too close to the body. (b) Holding it while reciting a prayer to God (i.e., for healing, prosperity, etc.). (c) Holding it next to the Chakras when linking with the energy of the meridians in your body.

Crystal 2 - Citrine: This crystal can be used during meditation for calming and centering your mind. Citrine is also beneficial to use in conjunction with Amethyst if you suffer from an autoimmune disorder such as Lupus or Scleroderma. Citrine is not recommended during pregnancy or breastfeeding since some information suggests that it may cause harm to the fetus if held close to the body.

This crystal has the ability to balance your emotions as well as the chakras. It can be used to end anger, fear, and rage.

Holding Citrine in meditation will help you eliminate negative emotions and replace them with positive ones. It's a beautiful crystal to use when addressing anger issues by visualizing that the anger is being drained from your body through the crown chakra. In addition, it's a wonderful crystal for confidence building and self-esteem enhancement during meditation since it can lift your self-confidence higher than where it was before you started meditating (even if you start out feeling low).

Some recommended visualization techniques with Citrine are (a) Holding it in meditation (i.e. imagine it filling your body with golden light and watch the color of your aura change to a brighter one), (b) placing it on your third eye (in order to increase psychic abilities), and (c) keeping it in a place where you spend time so that you can feel its energy.

Citrine is a powerful stone that possesses the qualities of courage, creativity, and wealth. Holding Citrine in meditation before making any important decisions will help you come up with solutions that are innovative and unique. You'll be able to think more clearly during stressful times when you use this crystal by using breathing exercises in addition to holding it during meditation. When placing Citrine in your home it will bring good luck and prosperity to your home and family members. This is especially helpful for those who wear Citrine jewelry or keep it near their personal belongings.

Citrine attracts love, unity, compassion, and happiness. It helps us realize our own self-worth and bring love into our lives. Citrine sharpens our intuition so that we can grow spiritually and expand our consciousness of who we are as a whole person. This crystal also helps us remember who we are from when times at work seem overwhelming or when we feel like giving up. It is particularly good for those who are struggling in the workplace. This crystal is also a wonderful stone to use during meditation, as it helps us to stay present in the moment and not dwell on the past or worry about future events.

Citrine can boost your confidence when you find yourself in challenging situations. It can also help those who feel insecure or lack self-esteem when working, studying, being intimate, or in any other situation that requires one to act confidently. Healing crystals such as Amethyst and Citrine are especially beneficial for anyone dealing with emotional issues or stress disorders since these crystals have a soothing effect on the mind and emotions. Citrine is also a wonderful stone to use anytime you want to release pent up anger, resentment, or rage. It can help heal damaged relationships by replacing negative feelings with positive ones.

Citrine is a powerful stone that promotes selflessness, and helps us learn how to love unconditionally. It allows us to have a more positive outlook on life, and helps us become the best version of ourselves. Citrine encourages happiness and joy in anyone who has been affected by depression or sadness.

Crystal 3 - Hyophorite: Considering how deeply connected we all are, it's no wonder this crystal can be used for depression and anxiety that stem from losing individual identity in the group (i.e. being labeled "the outcast"). One of the main reasons Hyophorite is used for this purpose is due to its ability to help us take responsibility for our own state of mind.

Crystal 4 - Citrine: This crystal can be used during meditation for calming and centering your mind. Citrine is also beneficial to use in conjunction with Amethyst if you suffer from an autoimmune disorder such as Lupus or Scleroderma. Citrine is not recommended during pregnancy or breastfeeding since some information suggests that it may cause harm to the fetus if held close to the body.

Crystal 5 - Aquamarine: This is the master healer for emotions. It can help overcome depression, anxiety, anger, stress, and create a more positive attitude toward life. Aquamarine is used in healing crystals because it has the power to balance the mind and emotions.

Meditation with Amethyst and Citrine enhances our ability to meditate with Aquamarine. If you already know how to do meditation then you can combine these three without any problems since they all have compatible energies.

When meditating with Aquamarine it will help you develop your intuition and psychic abilities. It can also help you relax, calm down, and eliminate stress. As a master healer for emotions, it's beneficial to use this during times of worry, anxiety and stress. It has also been known to help those who have difficulty communicating with others.

Aquamarine is a stone that brings peace of mind and emotional balance when used during meditation. It can be used in conjunction with Amethyst and Citrine when dealing with strong emotions such as grief or rage that's hard to control if left unchecked. This stone deals with emotions through bringing calmness into the mind and heart when we are angry or upset about something. It's beneficial to use for anyone who finds it hard to make their feelings known, or if they struggle with the feeling of being misunderstood. Aquamarine can help you express your feelings in a calm way, so the people around you will understand what you are trying to say. It's also beneficial for those who tend to bottle up their feelings and act out in unhealthy ways.

Crystal 6 - Blue Topaz: This crystal has been used in meditation for over 4,000 years by different civilizations around the world. It brings calmness into the mind and emotions when placed on the Third Eye Chakra during meditation.

Blue Topaz is a gentle stone that can help clear negative energy and heal emotional wounds. Blue Topaz balances all of the chakras, which makes it a great crystal for meditation. Its calming energy is beneficial to use when you need to clear your mind so you can think more clearly, or if you feel over-whelmed by emotion.

When used in meditation during bad times, Blue Topaz will bring calmness into your mind and bring peace to your heart. This crystal helps you release anger and negative emotions by turning them into positive ones. It's especially useful when dealing with difficult situations such as anger towards your partner or family members. Blue Topaz will help you to have healthier relationships by allowing you to forgive and move forward from the situation.

Blue Topaz is a stone that's used widely in crystal healing. It comes in many different colors, with Blue Topaz having the most beautiful and powerful energies. It can be used for healing not only emotional issues, but also physical ones such as acne, eczema, rashes, and digestive problems. Keep Blue Topaz on your body anytime you feel stress or anxiety building up so that it can help ease the symptoms of these conditions before they get out of hand. This is especially beneficial for those who suffer from severe anxiety or panic attacks that make it difficult to handle normal everyday activities.

Crystal 7 - Tedstone: This stone is good for overcoming fear and anxiety if held in any of the three major Chakras (i.e., crown, third eye, or solar plexus). It can also be used to help those who have been through a traumatic experience become more fearless. Tedstone will help you feel less fear during meditation by energizing your heart Chakra so it can open your heart and allow you to move beyond past trauma from your life.

Holding Tedstone in meditation will help you learn to accept your emotions and deal with them instead of hiding them inside or running away from them. When you are able to release emotion, it will grow stronger in the future. Tedstone can be used along with other crystals when meditating so that it can help bring the desired outcome faster.

CRYSTALS FOR GOAL SETTING AND ACHIEVEMENT

Do you have an important goal that has been hard to achieve? Have you ever found yourself constantly putting off and procrastinating? Do you often feel like giving up on your goals altogether? You are not alone. There is a method known as "mind programming" which will empower yourself to continue your quest for accomplishment.

7 Crystal for Goal Setting and Achievement: How They Work

The following crystals have been selected for their ability to help you achieve your goals in life. Goal setting is often a challenging task, mainly because it involves having the willpower to stick with your goal even when you feel like giving up or procrastinating. The following crystal will help you stay motivated when times get tough and also serve as an inspiration to keep moving forward:

1. Lapis Lazuli (aka Blue Sapphire)

Lapis is one of the most powerful crystals in terms of manifestation. It can also aid you in keeping your goals in check and on track. It's helpful for gaining confidence and power over any goals or challenges that you might be facing. This crystal will help you feel good about yourself, love yourself and accept who you are. The essence of lapis is to empower and give back to others, so it's a perfect stone for goal setting as well!

How To Use: Lapis is a very versatile stone, so it can be used in many ways. For example, you can carry a piece of lapis in your pocket or as a charm to set as a pendant.

You can also use this stone to help create an intention and visualize the outcome you want to achieve in life. Lapis should be used in conjunction with another crystal that will intensify its power, such as agate or sodalite.

2. Turquoise

This stone has been used by indigenous cultures for healing remedies for centuries. It can be used to help you gain confidence, as well as motivation, self-assurance and optimism about life and achieving your goals. It will also give you inner strength to do what's best and right, even when the going gets tough! Turquoise is also a stone of protection that will keep your energy clean and pure.

How To Use: You can carry a piece of turquoise with you at all times, or set it in your home or office to bring it some good energy. You can also use this crystal to create an intention for a more successful and fruitful career or business.

3. Topaz (any type)

This crystal has been used for centuries as a stone of success, power and strength. It can help you conquer your fears in order to achieve your goals. It is also helpful for those who want to increase their intuition or have a better understanding of the meaning of life. Topaz will help you tap into your creative abilities and expand your consciousness for a more fulfilling life.

How To Use: This stone should be placed on the Third-Eye Chakra area (between your eyes) or carried in order to be fully potent with its energies.

4. Yellow Calcite: Energy and Motivation

This crystal is associated with the solar plexus chakra, which is located on the upper abdomen. It's used for personal power, motivation, initiative and vitality. It will also help you overcome any fears you might have when it comes to achieving your goals in life. Yellow calcite is a great stone for strengthening mental powers, self-discipline and self-confidence. It will also help you set realistic goals and then gain the determination you need to achieve them.

How To Use: Carry a piece of yellow calcite with you at all times or set it in your home or office. Some people also like to use this stone along with other crystals that are associated with the solar plexus chakra, such as sugilite, amber and citrine.

5. Sugilite: Energy, Intuition and Awareness

This stone is used for bringing balance to the body's subtle energy system (chakras), as well as aiding in physical healing. It's used for developing psychic abilities and bringing more awareness into the physical realm so that one may expand their consciousness. It can also be used to help you overcome feelings of sadness and despair, as well as increase your motivation and determination to achieve your goals in life.

How To Use: Carry a piece of sugilite with you at all times or set it in your home or office. This stone should be used with another crystal that's associated with the Third-Eye Chakra, such as lapis lazuli or yellow calcite.

6. Rose Quartz: Love and Motivation

This is a wonderful crystal for helping you find love, which will in turn give you more energy and enthusiasm for achieving other goals in life. This crystal is also used to help ground you in the physical realm, and will also help you overcome negative emotions.

How To Use: Carry a piece of rose quartz with you at all times or set it in your home or office. You can also use this stone with other crystals that are associated with the Third-Eye Chakra, such as lapis lazuli or yellow calcite.

7. Black Tourmaline: Protection and Inner Strength

This crystal is used for strength, protection and bringing inner essence into the physical plane of existence – which means you'll be able to achieve more of what you want in life! It will also help strengthen your intuition, bring about courage and fortitude for personal achievement. Black tourmaline is also a powerful stone for those who have trouble dealing with their emotions, and will help you gain the strength to stand up for yourself.

How To Use: Carry a piece of black tourmaline with you at all times or set it in your home or office. This stone should also be used with another crystal that's associated with the Third-Eye Chakra, such as lapis lazuli or yellow calcite.

8. Green Tourmaline: Sense and Mindfulness

This crystal is known for bringing spiritual awareness into the physical realm, making it a great stone for meditation and self-reflection. It will also encourage the user to become more in tune with the world around them, and to create a sense of empathy with others.

How To Use: Carry a piece of green tourmaline with you at all times or set it in your home or office. This stone should also be used with another crystal that's associated with the Third-Eye Chakra, such as lapis lazuli or yellow calcite.

9. Aventurine: Attracting Wealth and Prosperity

This stone is used for attracting wealth, luck and prosperity into your life. It's also used for overcoming disappointment and for seeing the positive side of life. Aventurine will give you an outlet to express your creativity, and will clear out blockages that may be holding you back. It's a great stone for those who want to know how to heal depression fast.

How To Use: Carry a piece of aventurine with you at all times or set it in your home or office. This stone should also be used with another crystal that's associated with the Third-Eye Chakra, such as lapis lazuli or yellow calcite.

10. Rose Quartz: Awakening Intuition

Rose quartz is used for enhancing intuition. It opens all the chakras, and will help you bring your intuition to heart. Rose quartz is associated with unconditional love, and bringing balance into relationships. It will cleanse and heal any area that's been hurt or damaged in your body.

How To Use: Carry a piece of rose quartz with you at all times or set it in your home or office, along with a sapphire crystal (which is also associated with the Third Eye Chakra). You can also meditate while gazing into a mirror made of rose quartz; this can be especially helpful if you're trying to resolve relationship issues.

11. Selenite

This crystal is a powerful Third Eye Chakra healing tool that is best used when combined with other crystals or gemstones. It's a strong detoxifier and energy cleanser, making it an excellent tool for banishing negativity and stress. Try using selenite in combination with any of the other crystals on this list for an enhanced effect.

12. Goldstone

Goldstone balances all of your chakras, but its primary function is to enhance intuition and bring clarity of thought to the mind. It's often used in combination with other crystals to assist with healing.

13. Leopardskin Jasper

This crystal is a powerful Third-Eye Chakra healing tool that is best used when combined with other crystals or gemstones. It can help you achieve success, and also brings stability into every aspect of your life.

14. Dioptase and Pyrite: This is a combination of both Dioptase and Pyrite, which are both useful for chakra alignment and self-healing. This makes them excellent tools to use during meditation for guided visualizations that would benefit achieving personal goals and dreams!

15. Pyrite and Tourmaline: This is a combination of Pyrite, which is useful for chakra alignment and self-healing, with Tourmaline, which can be used to help bring in luck, money and prosperity into your life.

16. Blue Calcite: This crystal can be used to gain wisdom about a specific situation or issue in order to help you achieve your goals. It can also be used to help you be more present in the moment, which will allow you to tap into your intuition.

17. Amethyst: This is a powerful crystal that can be used for protection and helps you overcome any fears that may stop you from achieving your goals. It's also used for bringing wisdom into life, and overcoming disappointment and despair when it comes to life's hardships.

18. Chalcedony: This is a stone used for self-discovery and healing of all chakras! It can be used on its own, but it's also very helpful when

combined with other crystals that are associated with the Third-Eye Chakra, such as lapis lazuli or black tourmaline.

19. Sugilite: This crystal is a powerful Third Eye Chakra healing tool that is best used when combined with other crystals or gemstones. It will help you tap into your intuition, bring about more self-awareness and will allow you to be more in touch with the world around you.

20. Labradorite: This crystal can be used for increasing mindfulness and awareness, as well as bringing a deeper connection between yourself and others. It will also help you overcome any fears that may prevent you from achieving your goals in life.

21. Bloodstone: This is a powerful stone that helps you to gain strength and courage to take action and overcome fear. It will also keep your energy clean so that you can approach your goals with confidence and belief in yourself.

22. Citrine: This crystal can be used as an aid to meditation, or for increased self-discipline in order to achieve one's goals. It's also used for helping one overcome feelings of anger, jealousy, betrayal and resentment.

23. Smoky Quartz: This crystal is used to help with healing the physical body, as well as provide clarity of thought so that one can achieve a higher understanding of life's obstacles.

24. Obsidian: This crystal can be used to banish negative energy and replace it with positive vibrations. It can also be used to clear your mind and release any emotional blocks that might have been holding you back from achieving your goals.

25. White Quartz: This crystal is used for protection, peace, purity and cleansing the mind of negative thoughts that prevent you from being successful in life.

26. Calcite: This is a powerful Third-Eye Chakra healing tool that is best used when combined with other crystals or gemstones, such as selenite or moonstone. You can use it on its own or with other crystals to enhance your meditation and healing abilities.

27. Monazite: This crystal is used for bringing balance into the physical plane of existence, as well as balancing all the chakras within the body. It's a great stone for helping you overcome any fears you might have when it comes to achieving goals in life, as well as giving you more confidence when being assertive with others.

28. Bloodstone: This is a powerful stone that helps you to gain strength and courage to take action and overcome fear. It will also keep your energy clean so that you can approach your goals with courage, determination and belief in yourself.

29. Lepidolite: This crystal can be used to improve self-esteem and self-awareness, as well as help you overcome feelings of depression and unhappiness. You can also use this crystal in combination with other crystals that are associated with the Third Eye Chakra, such as lapis lazuli or yellow calcite.

30. Jasper: This crystal is known for helping to tackle any feelings of jealousy and resentment that are held within the heart chakra. It's also used for removing stagnant energy from a space, which creates greater support for your goals in life.

31. Labradorite: This stone is used for enhancing mindfulness and awareness, as well as bringing a deeper connection between yourself and others. It will also help you overcome any fears that may prevent you from achieving your goals in life.

32. Moonstone: This crystal is used for bringing love into your life, and it will also help you to overcome any feelings of depression or sadness that may be holding the heart chakra back from achieving its full potential.

33. Morganite: This crystal can bring about more self-confidence and self-esteem, as well as helping you to overcome feelings of jealousy and resentment. It can also be used to bring clarity into one's life so that one can achieve greater understanding of their emotions and how they affect their life choices.

34. Amethyst: This is a powerful crystal that can be used for protection and helps you overcome any fears that may stop you from achieving your goals. It's also used for bringing wisdom into life, and overcoming disappointment and despair when it comes to life's hardships.

35. Ruby: This stone is used for gaining wisdom and clarity of thought when it comes to making decisions that will help achieve one's goals in life. It's also used to help the user gain more confidence in their abilities, as well as help them overcome feelings of jealousy towards others who have accomplished what they want to achieve.

36. Sapphire: This stone can be used as a tool to allow you to see the bigger picture of your life, and can help you overcome any emotional blocks that prevent you from achieving your goals. It's also used for bringing a higher level of self-awareness, which is crucial in order to achieve success and happiness in life.

37. Rose Quartz: This crystal can be used for enhancing intuition, and allowing the user to tap into their creativity and see things more clearly when it comes to achieving their goals in life. You can also utilize this crystal on its own or with another crystal that's associated with the Third Eye Chakra, such as lapis lazuli or yellow calcite.

38. Hematite: This stone can help one to overcome any fears that prevent them from attaining their goals in life. It can also be used to increase energy and improve your stamina, as well as obtaining clarity of thought when it comes to achieving one's goals.

39. Fire Agate: This stone is used for bringing balance into the physical plane of existence, as well as balancing all the chakras within the body. It's a great stone for helping you overcome feelings of anger, jealousy and resentment.

40. Sodalite: This crystal can be used for helping you see the big picture when it comes to achieving one's goals in life. It can also be used to enhance confidence, as well as help one overcome feelings of depression and unhappiness.

10 THINKS TO AVOID WHEN WORKING WITH HEALING CRYSTALS

Thinks to Avoid When Working With Healing Crystal

1. Do not have negative thoughts about the crystal when you first work with it.

2. Allow your body to become accustomed to the presence of the stone before working with it for any length of time.

3. Work with only one stone at a time; do not mix crystals unless directed by a crystal therapist or experienced healer who knows how to combine certain stones together.

4. Keep your crystal clean and dry but be aware that some people find washing crystals can diminish their power so don't over wash them!

5. Keep your stones in an area where you spend a lot of time , such as on your nightstand, but be certain that it is in a place where it will not be knocked over or disturbed.

6. Keep the crystal more than six inches away from the TV and computer screen.

7. Do not wear crystals that are powerful for healing someone else; they are very personal and only meant to help you.

8. Work with only one type of stone at a time - for example, if you are working with a flower quartz crystal, do not use that same day a selenite or amethyst crystal! 9. Be aware that crystal energy is extremely powerful and it can give you results more quickly than other healing modalities if you are ready for change.

10. As with any new experience, be patient and trust your intuition during this transition period within.

Aventurine also works very well on the solar plexus chakra as it has been used for centuries to help balance and strengthen this center of our emotional body. It has been said to help one become more positive in their outlook on life while opening up the heart to give one a deeper and more profound ability to love self and others unconditionally.

Since the near-mythical acts of Jesus healing the sick, many cultures and religions have utilized crystals for their healing capabilities. Unlike other religions, however, many Jews do not practice using crystals to heal. As Judaism is a religion that emphasizes only using natural and scientific means to cure diseases.

Some of the things that must be avoided include:

1- Using crystals in one's home or space without clearing it first by a Rabbi or an accomplished spiritual leader who can guide you into connecting with your environment instead of it affecting you physically.

Using crystals, especially those that are new to you, as an alternative method to medical treatments. Some have argued that the placebo effect is stronger than the power of any crystal and that it is best to rely on Western medicine for all diseases. However, in cases where Western medicine cannot help, one may put his or her faith and trust into a Rabbi or spiritual leader who is capable of harnessing the power of crystals.

Wearing healing crystal energy jewelry as a fashion statement or treating it just as any other piece of jewelry (although many people choose to do so). Although many healers use jewelry to channel their powers, others believe that this practice can cause harm (especially if it was given to them by someone else).

Using a particular stone for healing when another would be more effective. However, there are some stones that have special mystical properties and can be dangerous to use on oneself or others without first clearing the environment around the person who is going to be healed.

Using crystals while in a state of emotional or physical distress. This practice can cause the strong energy of the crystal to direct itself into one's body in an unhealthy way, as if it were mistaking one's body for a crystal and attempting to heal it in the same way that it would heal any other piece of jewelry or implement (see point 1 and 2 above).

Using the power of crystals without understanding their proper ritual and ceremony. Crystals are often used in other cultures as symbols of great power and healing, but Judaism has evolved such that it relies only on natural remedies. Ancient cultures that relied solely on crystals were not aware of how to properly harness the power of these stones so they often caused harm to themselves or others.

Using crystals to perform voodoo-like rituals in an attempt to prolong life or bring revenge against those who have wronged you. Often, voodoo rituals use objects of ritual with which one would normally be in contact (such as a knife) when taking part in a healing session. Even if one does not intend to perform such a ritual, the ritual itself can be an aspect of voodoo, causing harm to oneself or others.

Using crystals in inappropriate rituals. A person attempting to use a crystal in an inappropriate way may harm himself or others by holding it in a non-professional way, such as exposing it directly to his body or allowing the other person in the room to hold it without proper guidance and energy clearing.

Using crystals while drunk or under the influence of drugs. The effects of alcohol and mood altering drugs can change one's actions when using crystal energy and lead him to engage in inappropriate actions (see point 2 above).

Using crystal energy for frivolous reasons such as entertainment or amusement. Would one use a knife to play with paper? Do you throw a rock in the ocean or firecrackers at the sky just because they are fun? Although crystals sometimes have an interesting appearance and wonderful properties (see point 3 above), these priceless stones should be used only to heal and not to be used in trivial acts of entertainment.

Using crystals when there is no need to do so, such as when one is feeling fine and does not need healing.

Using crystals that are too powerful for one's level of expertise. Although it is important to use an appropriate level of crystal power, there are occasions in which one may choose to use a more powerful crystal rather than the weaker ones. However, this practice can cause harm if the energy of the more powerful item is not properly controlled as it can be mistaken as a problem and cause harm to oneself or others.

Using crystals in rituals with other people who do not have a proper grasp on their energy and spiritual work. This can lead to confusion and even death if done by inexperienced individuals (see points 1 through 5).

Using crystals in rituals meant for other people (as opposed to your own body or environment). By using someone else's crystals, one can unintentionally cause harm to him or her.

Using crystals for entertainment purposes. Some people believe that it is okay to use the power of stones in this way, although they also believe it inappropriate to use any form of energy (including their own bodies) in this way.

Using crystals when there is not a need for them (e.g., when walking around the store without a purpose). Some believe that this practice is unhealthy for the person carrying the stone and can cause him or her to become confused about the purpose of his or her life.

Using crystals in a disrespectful manner. People who are not familiar with the proper respect given to crystals during healing sessions may cause harm to themselves by mishandling or using these stones improperly (see points 1 through 5).

Following your instincts about a specific crystal without first checking it out. There are occasions in which a person might buy an item and think that he is being guided in some way by his spiritual side only to later discover that this particular item was selected because of its rarity and monetary value rather than because of any real mystical value.

Not owning any crystals at all. Although some believe that it is beneficial to own a few crystals for use in rituals, other people believe that a person's psychic abilities can only be developed with practice and not by simply possessing objects. Some believe this to be quite ridiculous as if one did not have any energy in his or her body how could he or she possibly develop these skills?

Not knowing how to properly cleanse and use one's items. In this way, careless behavior during the cleansing process may cause negative consequences for the person performing the ritual.

Using less than 100% pure crystals (e.g., using stones which are slightly cloudy or colored with a spot of crystal dust). Sometimes people think that certain crystals or gems may not be of the highest quality but will nevertheless work for them. In many cases, this is true; however, some people forget that a less than 100% pure crystal is still a highly concentrated form of energy and may have unintended consequences on one's life if used in a ritual.

Using large amounts of crystals in one place at one time. One must be careful when using large quantities of stones as it can cause more confusion than clarity. People who are financially stable and are able to afford it may buy items to suit their every need; however, everyone else should use caution when using large numbers of stones at once as they may not be able to handle the energy released from these products.

- Wearing jewelry which is too heavy. This should never be done. Ashanti, who was a queen in Africa, once wore a necklace with over 3400 beads. Although this may have seemed like a marvelous way to celebrate her role as an African queen, it was also very dangerous for her to wear such an awesome piece of jewelry. However, knowing how precious Ananda's crystals were she still wore them even though she was afraid the weight they created would cause her to collapse during her meditations and rituals with them. The weight of the jewelry she wore was so heavy that it caused her to die several years before her time.

Intentionally infusing crystals with negative energy or negative entities. If a crystal is filled with negative energy, use candle magic to remove the negativity and fill it with positive energy instead. If you suspect a stone has been filled by an evil force or entity, contact a professional immediately!

Meditating while wearing jewelry which contains stones (e.g., bracelets and necklaces). It can be done but one must take precaution when doing so. It is recommended that you wear the stones on one arm only. This will avoid placing any pressure on the other arm which could create a connection between the two.

Without any doubt, crystal healing and stone therapy has experienced a significant surge in recent years. A multitude of people have found the practices to be effective tools for healing, self-awareness, and personal growth. It is no wonder that these stones are some of the most popular objects used in alternative medicine. However, when working with crystals or stones it is important to keep certain things in mind. While some of these points will not apply to everyone, taking precautions is never a bad idea.

Be Mindful of Your Intentions When Using Healing Stones and Crystals

This is especially important for those attempting to use stones for healing or therapy. If you want the stone or crystal to act as a conduit for energy and healing, tell it so. If you want the stone to focus on providing insight into your personal life, be clear about it. The more clearly you imagine what the crystal should do for you, the better chance it has of doing just that. It is okay if your desires are vague at first; with time your intentions will evolve and become clear. Ideally, you will be in harmony with the crystal or stone and both of you will have a positive experience.

Be Mindful of Where You Keep Your Stones and Crystals

The way you treat stones is indicative of the type of energy that they will provide for you. If your stones are kept on display, then they may project a powerful energy outward. It is not recommended that you keep these crystals in such places where their energy may be overstimulating or even disruptive to others. On the other hand, if you store your stones away from everyday life and packed away in boxes or storage areas, there is less of a chance that they will impact others in a positive way.

Avoid Storing Crystals or Stones When the Moon Is Full

There is an old, folklore saying that it is not a good idea to store your stones near the moon because this can cause them to become unstable. While this would seem to be an irrational idea, there is some truth to it. During full moons, there are more powerful and intense energies that can destabilize the stones and alter their properties for someone else. If you have a full moon in the night when you are storing crystals or stones with no other open spaces in your apartment, then it may be best to put these away for a while before you start using them again. You can place them somewhere safe for a few days before actually bringing them out once again.

Avoid Bringing Your Stones or Crystals Into Contact With Other Metals

In general, it is always a good idea to avoid exposing your stones and crystals to other metals because this can have an adverse effect on their properties. Such exposure can make the stone more vulnerable to outside energies that can change the way it feels and works for you. It is also important to keep your stones away from magnets. The magnetic charge will have an effect on the stone and this will weaken its overall potency.

Be Mindful of Where You Obtain Your Crystals From

This goes beyond where you purchase them, though this is certainly a consideration as well. It is also about how they were obtained. If you are buying them from a place that was mining for them versus one that actually harvested and carved them out of the earth, this will affect their overall power. In general, it is best to get your stones from places where they were harvested and carved because this way you can be sure of their authenticity.

Avoid Using Stones and Crystals That Are Lying on the Ground

It might seem like common sense to not pick up rocks or stones off the ground for fear of contamination or other negative things, but this advice goes well beyond this. If you are using healing crystals or stones for meditation purposes, it is a good idea to cleanse them before use. It is not safe to have stones that are already contaminated when you might be holding them in your hands. To avoid this, simply place them into a bowl of water or a bucket of sand before you use them.

Avoid Using Stones and Crystals That Have Been Doused With Other Substances

Not only is this bad practice but it will also damage the power of the stone or crystal. In some cases, the stone may become more unstable because it has been weakened by exposure to other substances. If you want to cleanse a stone, then cover it in a small amount of alcohol and allow it to sit for a few hours. This will help to strip off any contaminates that may have been doused on the stone and leave it in a state where it can be used for healing.

HOW TO MANTAIL CRYSTALS AND JEWELRY

Manteling is a process by which quartz crystals are grown or obtained from rock using heat and pressure. The reasons for performing manteling depend on the intended use of the crystal. For example, it might be used in jewelry to increase its stability

The best way to learn how to mantel crystals, therefore, is through practice and experimentation. Ask your jeweler about any particular types of methods they use when shaping your stone before you try them yourself. It's better to rely on a professional rather than attempt something haphazardly without knowing what could happen in the process.

Manual methods can be used with any type of quartz or beryl ore. These stones are often mined directly from the ground, although they can also be artificially grown or made in a laboratory. Typically the preferred material to grow through manual manteling is amethyst, which is also the easiest stone to start working with due to its transparency.

If you are using a natural rock crystal, you will likely need to start with a large one that has already been partially shaped. This will make your job easier than trying to shape an entire piece from scratch.

Steps for Manual Methods of Manteling (Pre-Polishing)

Most quartzers start by filling a large pot with water for soaking the gathered quartz crystals. It is best to use pure distilled water, as chemicals in tap water are highly likely to damage your crystals or even make them less stable.

After the crystals have completely soaked, they should be moved into a place where you can hold them in an upright position. Quartz has a natural inclination to be curved, so it can take some time to shape the first stone into an appropriate profile. There are many ways you can do this; try working gradually over different sized stones before settling on one structure that works best for all of them.

Once a shape has been determined, use a variety of tools to work the stone into a tight, polished form. Simple tools such as sandpaper or a belt sander can do the job quickly. A more advanced method is called polishing. This involves using files and other abrasive tools for finer detail work.

After you have finished with most of the rock, you will need to move the stones back into the water for another soak. Leave them in there long enough to dry completely and then handle them again for another round of shaping and polishing. Depending on the texture of the stone, you may need to soak it several times before it is ready.

Curved quartz crystals can be manually shaped by heating them up until they are soft and pliable. This method is best suited for smaller stones that have already been partially shaped, but can also be used with larger stones to enhance their stability or facilitate fixing a cracked piece together.

To manually shape the rock into a curve using heat, you will need a kiln pre-set to 1200 degrees Fahrenheit. For safety reasons, make sure that your kiln has an automatic temperature sensor before starting this process. There should also be someone else in the room to turn off the grates if needed.

Once the rock is inside the kiln, it will take about an hour to heat up. Once it has reached 1200 degrees, you can begin bending the crystal into the appropriate position. Since quartz is brittle, you will need to use a rubber mallet or some other tool for applying pressure. You should also wear gloves while handling hot quartz crystal.

When you are done, put another kiln setting on your kiln that slowly drops the temperature back to room temp over an extended period of time (8-10 hours). This helps stabilizes the stone and insures that it will not crack under normal conditions. It should be noted that some quartz crystals may be damaged if they are left in the kiln too long, so be careful!

Cooling Methods and Designs for Quartz Crystals

Crystal cooling is, as the name implies, a process by which you cool down your quartz crystal to help it stabilize and grow. There are two basic ways to do this; the first involves heating up the crystal and putting it back in water or ice. The second method is to physically place the stone in a freezer or refrigerator.

When you are cooling your stones, make sure that they do not become frozen solid. The cooling process should be done very slowly so that your crystal is not damaged. When you are ready to place your quartz stone into the freezer, the temperature should be set at about 40 degrees Fahrenheit.

Some people put a small amount of water in the freezer along with their crystals, so that they will freeze onto a base of ice rather than become stuck to another part of the freezer. When it comes time to remove your stones from the cold environment, make sure that you do so gradually rather than letting them sit out at room temperature for a long period of time before returning them to their normal environment.

Crystals should be stored at temperatures below 5 degrees Celsius to prevent them from cracking or breaking.

Returning Your Crystal to Its Natural Environment

When you are done working with your rock, the best thing to do is return it to its natural environment. This may mean returning it into the ground, but a better idea is to set it on a flat surface that keeps direct sunlight away from it if possible. This will help slow down the growth process and prevent any further damage to your crystal's delicate center.

Quartz crystals are used for many different applications in the jewelry industry, especially those related to healing and metaphysical practices. Since quartz is made up from silicon dioxide, it does not occur in its pure form in nature.

Quartz crystal is used to make some types of microprocessors, because it can process signals very quickly. Because of this, quartz crystals are commonly used in computers and other electronics devices. Quartz crystal is also being used to make speakers for audio equipment used on televisions and computers. It can also be found in car radios and cell phones.

Since quartz crystal stores energy so well, it is used as a power source for various types of electronics such as watches and calculators. Quartz crystals are also commonly used for the oscillating movement inside clocks, watches and timers.

Quartz crystal can be found in many different sizes, and they are often used to make pendants, necklaces or other types of jewelry. Many people believe that carrying quartz crystals with them or wearing them as jewelry can help to prevent illness, pain and help promote overall good health.

The healing powers of quartz crystals are well known by many people around the world. Healers are able to use quartz crystals to influence a person's energy field, even if they are not in the same room as the stone.

As a result, quartz crystals are commonly used in Reiki healing practices and other forms of holistic medicine.

Crystals are also commonly used for metaphysical purposes as well. These crystals are able to act as an amplifier or detector in order to pick up energy. It can often be used to draw certain energy from one place and send it elsewhere. Crystals are also commonly used for healing purposes. These include treatment for things like headaches, stress, tiredness and depression. Quartz is also commonly used in crystal healing practices as a form of protection against psychic attack and negative entities.

Quartz crystals are an incredible form of protection, especially for people who may have peculiar patterns on their auric field or who have some other type of energy blockage pattern within their aura field. Quartz crystals are able to cleanse and clear out this blockage so that it can be released. Quartz crystal also helps to protect you from negative energy, or even psychic attack as well.

Quartz crystals are also used in white magic practices. They are used to influence people and objects in a positive manner, and they can be used to remove negative energies as well. They can also help to banish various kinds of negative entities from your environment like ghosts, demons or other types of evil spirits. Crystals are also commonly used for cleansing purposes so that the boundaries around your property can be cleansed of various types of negative energies.

Crystals can also be used in order to influence what you are working on. If you are doing some type of psychic development or even trying to develop your own type of white magic, the use of crystal can greatly aid you in this process. Crystals themselves are very powerful and they can create certain energies that can help to attract other positive energies which helps aid in manifestation. In addition, crystals also provide a type of grounding energy so that you do not get overwhelmed with the energies that you are working on.

Quartz crystal is really an incredible gemstone, and it has many different types of purposes that it is used for. There are many different types of quartz crystals that you can find in nature, and most of these are very powerful. Quartz crystal is one of the most powerful gemstones that you can ever find, and this is known for its energy as well as the healing properties associated with it. There are certain types of crystals that help to focus on certain types of energy that will be helpful for your manifestation process.

When using quartz crystals to aid in your manifestation process, you must learn how to use these crystals properly so that they will give you the maximum benefit. Using quartz crystals in conjunction with other stones is a great way to manifest a lot faster. Crystals like black tourmaline can be used in combination with quartz crystals so that you can increase the power of the quartz stone while also clearing out any negative energy.

You can also use obsidian in conjunction with quartz crystals as well. Obsidian is a volcanic glass that is very sharp and it will cut through any kind of negativity or lower frequency energy. It will clear out any type of psychic attack or blockages that you might have as well, and it is often used in order to protect your auric field from negative entities. Crystals like hematite are also another good stone to use with quartz crystals, because hematite helps to ground them and prevent them from being too overpowering.

The crystal field around your home can be an issue, and this can make it so that you are unable to manifest what you desire. Crystals like amethyst can help to clear out this type of negativity, and they will also increase the energy around your property in order to aid with manifestation.

Be careful with these crystals when you are working with them because they are very powerful stones, and they can easily damage your aura field if you are not careful. If you suspect that negative energies are coming into your home or property, then it is best to use the protection properties of these stones first before moving on and trying to manifest something.

Crystals are able to absorb energy quite readily, and they can be used in order to store energy as well. If you want something to stay with you for a long time, then quartz crystal is the best option. It will help store the energy so that it can manifest in your life whenever you need it.

Mantel crystals and jewelry can vary in size, material, color, and style. Some are perfect for casual wear while others are for formal events. All of them have detailed instructions about how to mantel the piece on your own.

Here are a few tips from experienced mantelers:

-Glass is a lot heavier than plastic so use caution when trying to mantel it. Glass also does not flex as much as plastic so if you want to use it in an area where space is limited like an office cubicle, be sure to get the appropriate size of hook for its height or else it may fall down and break upon rotating around the rod.

Garnet is a great choice for most mantels because it has a nice depth and richness to it. It is even better if you can get it in a variety of colors because the colors will add more dimensions to your piece.

Mixed metals are also quite attractive because they are mixed together by the artist as opposed to just being bolted in place. They are always at least 3 different metals in one piece so you can tell they were crafted with care and great attention to detail.

Swarovski Crystals come in many sizes, shapes, and styles. They have very good size and weight that makes them easy to mantel without any problems. The small ones are about half an inch or a little more while the large ones are about 4 inches. They also have a nice sparkle that adds lots of shine to mantels.

Antique jewelry is usually very beautiful and quite popular in the mantel community. It can be made from silver, gold, or platinum metal and is often set with beautiful diamonds, rubies, sapphires, or other precious stones. Not all antique pieces are practical for manteling because they might have delicate settings that will not allow them to endure the process of putting them up on a rod. The artist will usually put this information in the description of the item before you buy it so be sure to read it carefully if you still want to mantel a piece of antique jewelry.

Crystal is a very popular choice for manteling and it comes in different types such as glass, crystal quartz, aquamarine, or a variety of other beautiful stones. Crystal quartz is made up of many colors that all shine brightly under direct light. They look like they are lit from within and really add shine to any room or wall they are placed on.

No matter what you choose to do with your mantel, be sure to use caution when moving it about as not to drop or break it because of its weight and size. A good mantel will last a lifetime and look just as good, if not better than the day you bought it so be sure to take care of yours by keeping it clean, dusting regularly, and adding any new pieces of crystal or jewelry to it every now and then. Mantels are not only beautiful, but also very versatile. They can be used to display different jewelry and decorations or to hold larger pieces of crystal that would have been too big for a table, desk, or counter in the past. They have come a long way since the day they were first hung and now there are many different styles, colors, and shapes to choose from. They are great for any room in the house or business office and would be a great addition to any décor.

Sewing crystals into cloth, fiber, or other products is a very old tradition. Examples of this are shown in the textile collections in the National Museum of African Art (Washington). "Mossi" ceremonial robes are manteled with cloth mantels covered with sewn and appliquéd gold nuggets, each one representing a fetish. One type of cotton mantel in Mali is called "koyik" and is made of multicolored cloth with appliquéd seed beads and sewn-on ribbons depicting animals, gods, proverbs, wishes for good luck, etc. These pieces go back to at least 600 B.C.E. in African art and most likely beyond that.

Mantel crystals and jewelry have been around for thousands of years as well, dating back to ancient times such as the Egyptian. Many Egyptian artifacts have mantels placed on them such as busts and statues. The Egyptians made their mantels out of gold, silver, or other precious jewels. They would also often put a single crystal on each mantel to add more shine and beauty to it. Ancient Egyptians were very well known for their craftsmanship when it came to mummification so they definitely knew what they were doing when they created these pieces.

CRYSTALS FROM A-Z

Crystals are beautiful and often powerful minerals, but they're not just for show—they can have innumerable healing powers. They can enhance your mood, balance your chakras, help you sleep better and more soundly, while also clearing physical pain. Here is a list of crystals beginning with the letter A to Z that will refresh your memory of their amazing properties and healings!

A - Amethyst: The fact that Amethyst has the ability to mitigate negative emotions is what makes it a popular stones for meditation in lieu of other translucent crystals like Turquoise or Lapis-Lazuli. The soothing color and energy of Amethyst has been known to promote a sense of contentment, and it can help with anger, irritability, restlessness, lethargy, pain and more.

Amethyst also encourages psychic abilities and the crown chakra in particular. If you're seeking spiritual healing but have trouble reaching that level of peace where you can hear your higher self or deity communicating with you, Amethyst's energy may help bridge the gap. It's also a powerful component in layouts for manifestation or dream-attainment.

B - Blue Calcite: Blue Calcite is a powerful tool for communication on all levels. This translucent, cerulean stone is wonderful for opening the Throat Chakra, which makes it ideal for public speaking. It's also great for writers as it helps protect against writer's block, and can help one start a writing project by allowing the words to flow freely from one's pen or tongue.

Blue Calcite can also be used to attract inspiration from your higher self or deity, making it helpful when seeking new ways of solving problems in your life. It can de-stress an overworked mind in the same way Amethyst does. Naturally soothing and calming, Blue Calcite is also believed to bring prosperity into one's life, making it an excellent stone to use during layouts involving wealth-attainment.

C - Citrine: Though this deep orange gem is an excellent stone for enhancing the mood, Citrine also has healing properties. It's been known to help relieve stress, encourage mental clarity and even stimulate energy in the physical body.

Citrine is a powerful stone of manifestation between the eyebrows, and it encourages one to be more decisive in their actions. It can also help people focus on "the right thing," no matter how complicated a situation may seem. This makes Citrine a popular stone to use as part of layouts for business success or financial prosperity.

D - Diamond: Diamonds are known for their ability to strengthen the physical body and promote purity of thought and action. Used mostly for negative energy clearance, this crystal can be used to help clear out past emotional baggage and negative relationships. It's also known to be protective against psychic attacks.

E - Emerald: Emerald is a stone that enhances the heart chakra with an incredible sense of compassion and unconditional love for all living things. It's also a powerful emotional balancer, so if you're feeling out of balance in any way, or find that your emotions are getting the best of you from time to time, this is an excellent stone to use in meditation or during layouts for healing purposes.

Emerald is an excellent stone for attracting luck, abundance and prosperity into one's life, so it works well with layouts involving financial success or business growth. Emerald is also known to trigger creativity, and for those challenged by writer's block, it can help inspire you to put the words on paper.

F - Fluorite: Though this metallic blue crystal is known for its ability to eliminate radiation from the body, it also has quite a few other uses. Fluorite is a powerful balancing stone that can be used in layouts for healing purposes or during meditation to bring your energy back into alignment.

Fluorite is also known to amplify one's intellect, making it an excellent stone for students. It's especially helpful in the areas of math and science. Fluorite can also assist in manifestation, and it's believed to help one develop their psychic abilities.

G - Garnet: Garnet is a powerful stone that encourages one to aim high, set goals that are outside of their comfort zone and then go after them with passion. Though success may not always come as fast as we'd like it too, this is an empowering stone that will help one persevere through any challenges they may face along the way.

Garnet is also an excellent stone during layouts for manifestation, as it will help you focus on what exactly it is that you want, and not just how you want your life to be better. It's a crystal that can help one stay focused on their goals and provides a much-needed energy boost when one begins to doubt themselves or the goals they've set.

H - Hematite: Hematite is the perfect stone for people seeking protection from negative influences in their lives. This black stone will curb any negativity and replace it with an elevated sense of confidence, optimism and willpower.

Hematite is a powerful grounding stone that can help to release any negative energies that may be stuck in your aura. This makes it an excellent stone to use in layouts for healing, as well as layouts involving manifestation or prosperity. It will also bring one's physical body back into balance, which can be helpful during layouts involving health issues.

I - Iolite: Iolite is a crystal that promotes the development of intuition, and it helps open up the Crown Chakra, allowing one to receive information from higher levels of consciousness. It also encourages deeper spiritual growth and understanding by helping you connect with your inner soul, or divine self.

J - Jasper: Jasper is an excellent tool for enhancing one's ability to manifest their goals, as it helps to clear emotional blocks that may be standing in the way of positive change. Those who are motivated by passion in their lives will find that using jasper while meditating on a goal will help them stay focused and committed to their cause.

K - Kyanite: This Gemstone will help manifest one's goals during layouts that are related to building, and it will aid in the manifestation of new ideas as well. It's beneficial for people of all ages, including children who want to learn more about cause and effect. It can also balance the chakras, so it's a great stone to use when a student is struggling with balancing their lives while going through school.

L - Lapis Lazuli: Lapis Lazuli is excellent for helping one remain calm and focused in any situation they find themselves in, so it's a great stone for layouts involving leadership or group work. Lapis Lazuli works well with all gemstones, and it can be used in layouts for manifestation, prosperity, protection and all other areas of life.

Lapis is one of the most powerful stones for manifesting one's goals during a layout. It has energy that can quickly tap into any situation and help you to see the best possible outcome in the present moment. Many people believe that Lapis Lazuli magically brings about what it was placed upon, so it's important to be mentally prepared for what you want to happen throughout your layouts.

M - Moonstone: This stone, also known as "The Magician's Stone," helps one see things from a more compassionate perspective during layouts, which can help people achieve their goals with more ease. It's all about harmony, and it can be used for manifestation, protection, money and so much more. It is a very versatile stone that can be used for any reason one needs to use a stone for.

Moonstone is primarily used as a way to manifest what one wants to have in their life. It helps you see the bigger picture, so it can be used for any layout that involves manifesting what one wants or needs. Moonstone can also be placed on the Thymus Chakra and the Heart Chakra to help clear out any negative emotions that may be causing you issues in your life.

N - Nephrite: This stone is known as "The Peace Stone" and it's a great choice for layouts involving communication with others, whether it's expressing oneself verbally or non-verbally. It helps alleviate stress and will enhance the energy of the other stones in the layout.

O - Obsidian: This stone is used to remove anything that isn't serving you, including old energies, negative thoughts or emotions, and bad habits. It's best left to be placed directly over the Root Chakra. It's also known as "The Protector Stone."

P - Pearl: This stone is primarily used for love layouts. It not only enhances the energy of other stones in a layout, but it will also attract new love into your life. Pearls are also very useful in layouts where divination is needed.

Q - Quartz Crystal: This crystal is used to eliminate anxiety and stress from one's life. It is also said to dissolve and clear negativity between people so that others cannot use your energy against you. Tiger Eye assists one in finding their life purpose and in focusing one's energy on this purpose. It relieves fear and worry, a useful crystal to have when one is undergoing any kind of treatment for cancer, or before making important decisions. Use Tiger Eye to enhance creativity and encourage imagination, it will also help you to find answers by providing a clear perspective on problems or issues that are faced by you.

R - Rose Quartz: Rose Quartz is considered to be one of the most powerful crystals for healing. It is a beautiful stone for helping you be your best self and promoting healing. Once it's placed on the Heart Chakra, it can be used to raise yin energy for those who are struggling with being fully present in their life or tasks they are working on. When used in layouts, Rose Quartz can help one see things from a higher perspective and can aid in letting go of any negative beliefs or emotions that may have been holding them back from being their best selves.

S - Selenite: Selenite is a wonderful stone for healing, as it will clear away any negative energy that has built up in one's system. It's mostly useful for healing layouts that focus on the Chakras. This crystal is useful when placed on the Throat Chakra to help release pent up anger or frustration, or on the Heart Chakra to assist one with saying what was left unsaid.

Selenite can also be used during layouts for manifestation, as it will help one stay focused and committed to their goals throughout the entire process. Meditation with Selenite will also enhance one's inner sight and sense of intuition to help you better understand your spiritual path.

T - Tiger Eye: A stone of protection, Tiger Eye is believed to bring about a sense of clarity and confidence. It's especially useful when one is dealing with negative emotions that may be holding them back in some way. This stone also helps one stay focused on their tasks throughout the day, so it's a great crystal for those who work in a high-stress environment and need help staying motivated during the day.

This crystal can also be used to enhance the energy between two people at work or in a relationship, as it will help them stay focused on each other during challenging times. Tiger Eye is a stone that can quickly clear away negative energy from one's aura, making it an excellent tool for clearing negative energy.

U - Unakite: An excellent grounding stone for those who want to manifest success in their lives. It will help you stay focused and motivated, so this crystal is best used with layouts that require high levels of determination and perseverance. This crystal works well with manifestation, prosperity and all other areas of life as well.

V - Vanadinite: One of the best stones for working with the Throat Chakra and overcoming emotional blocks in life. It will help you unleash yourself as a leader and be able to make changes in your life from the heart. It's also an excellent stone for manifesting one's goals during layouts, so it works well with layouts involving prosperity, love and all other areas of life.

W - White Agate: This stone is excellent for calming emotions on a physical level. It can also be used to enhance forgiveness when anger arises from someone else's actions, as well as one's own actions towards others. Use this stone when you want to take care of both sides of an argument or disagreement, so that each person can feel their needs have been met without feeling threatened by anyone else involved in the situation.

White Agate is also known as "The Healer's Stone," and it is used to stimulate the Root Chakra, which improves the flow of chi throughout one's system. It can also be used during layouts for manifestation, creativity and overall healing.

X - Xenotime: This is considered to be one of the most powerful stones for healing in existence. It is also a powerful stone for manifestation and prosperity. It will help one to see the big picture and will give you a better understanding of what exactly it is that you want in your life. Use Xenotime during layouts when you have difficulty communicating with others, and it can also be used to attract wealth into your life.

Y - Yellow Topaz: This crystal can help one manifest their dreams into reality, as well as enhance any manifestation process during a layout or meditation session. Yellow topaz can be placed anywhere throughout the body, but is most effective when placed on the Heart Chakra.

Z - Zincite: This stone has protective properties that can expel negative energy from one's body and aura, and it helps remove any negative energies that may be interfering with one's luck. This stone is a powerful stone for removing negative thoughts, and it also helps with intuition. It can be placed over the Crown Chakra to help you get in touch with your inner soul or divine self, and it can also be used to enhance the energy of other stones during a layout.

HOW TO CREATE A CRYSTALS GRID

Crystal grids are a way of arranging crystallized minerals, poppets, and other items in order to channel healing power. They can be used for a variety of purposes, from mental clarity to tulip cultivation! Here's how you can make one.

1. Gather your crystals and tools   - You'll need crystals with at least one flat side that is large enough for you to draw on there: quartz points or arrowheads work well; small bits of obsidian come in handy as well. Other tools include a paintbrush or straws for drawing out the grid lines, and any items (poppets or herbs) that will go into the grid with the crystals.

2. Choose an appropriate time and place   - Choose an appropriate time and place for this work. In some traditions, crystal grids are cast at night, while others cast during the waxing moon. If you are uncertain of the timing, look to your intuition or ask your magical guides for help.

3. Perform a grounding and centering exercise - perform a grounding and centering exercise before beginning: This will help you keep yourself in the moment as well as protect your energy field from being drained by overuse or by forming unintentional connections with others' grids.

4. Draw a grid over the chosen space   - First you will want to find a place for your crystals. You can set them up anywhere you like, but keep in mind that the energy field of the quartz points or arrowheads will be most effective if they are in a particular spot. If you are using poppets or other items to go into the grid, you will want to make sure that these objects can fit easily into the space, and that no one object is placed too close to another.

5 . Center yourself, and then draw your first crystal line - Once you feel centered, bring your focus down to each crystal point and recite a charging chant. You can charge the points with your own energy, or use the power of your crystals. You can also charge them with specific intentions. In order for you to draw a line between two points, you must be able to see them both clearly before you begin drawing there - that is, it is not a place where the crystal points merge into one another or disappear into each other.

6. Draw a second line between those two points   - Then draw a second line between those two points using a different color of chalk if desired (this will help you visualize where each point has been placed).

7. Remove any unwanted lines   - The next step is to draw in any unwanted lines that still need to be eliminated. You can do this by drawing a simple line around the entire grid, or you can draw lines waiting for each missing piece (these should be drawn first).

8. Don't be surprised if the line between points disappears or jumps around ... - Once you've finished drawing in your lines, don't be surprised if some of them disappear entirely, or may feel as though the points are moving about rather than staying in one place. This happens because crystals ideally follow their own polarity (the tendency to move toward positive charge or away from negative charge). This is why it is often recommended to place a quartz point (or other crystal) on the opposite side of the energy flow in order to ground it.

9. Make sure that no lines cross each another - Check over your grid to ensure that all lines are arranged freely and do not cross or intersect.

10. Decide where you will place your poppets or herbs   - Once you have completed the grid, decide where you would like to place your poppets or herbs, as well as any other items that you may want included in the grid arrangement. Make any additional markings as needed.

11. Begin working with the grid   - When you are ready to begin, recall your intentions, center yourself, and focus down to each point one at a time. You can also charge the crystal points by connecting them through lines of light. Or you can simply visualize healing energy flowing into the grid as you look at each point.

12. Remove the grid when its purpose has been fulfilled - When you have finished working with your grid, make sure that there is nothing left in it, and try to return it to its original state (if applicable). However, you may want to leave your grid up for a few days before removing it. This way any remaining energy will move back into the crystals, or into the earth.

13. Give thanks and ground yourself - When you have finished, perform another grounding and centering exercise. You may also want to give thanks to the elements of nature and any spirits that may have been involved in this spellwork for their assistance in making this spell effective.

Additional Notes: 1) Crystal grids are usually placed on a flat surface in an area where no one will walk over them (such as on top of your altar). If you will be working with a larger grid, or you need to move it to clean around it, then you can use cloths to cover the crystal points. This way you can take the cloths off and then put them back on as needed without needing to relocate each crystal point every time.

2) If a large number of people are working with a grid (including those who are not skilled in magick), then it is best if only one person draws out the grid with crystals. It is also recommended that this person work at their own pace and not try to compete with anyone else's efforts.

3) When using pre-made grids, remember that these grids have been created for a specific purpose. Therefore you should only use them for that purpose - to place your crystals. If you wish to use a pre-made grid while working on another type of spell, then you may want to re-make the grid from scratch yourself.

4) While working with crystal grids we recommend that you do not move the grid around once it has been placed, as some of your energy will move away from the crystals as they are moved. However, if it helps guide your energy movement, then it is acceptable to move the grid in order to clean around it.

5) Remember, when placing the grid you can move one crystal point at a time, or all of them at once. However, if you choose to use the same order and placement every time, then there is no need to move any of the crystals in that area - simply place your new crystals into the template that already exists.

6) While working with crystal grids it is best not to become involved with other types of spells (such as candle magick or spell crafting). Even if your intention is not to mix magical styles they can interfere with each other nevertheless.

7) Remember, when you are working with crystal grids, that it can take a few minutes for them to come into effect. Please wait this time so that all your energy can be absorbed by the crystals.

8) If at any time you feel that your energy is too strong for the area or environment, or if you are unsure what effects the atmosphere has on you while working with crystal grids, then please break the connection from your crystals before attempting to continue.

9) You may wish to use an attunement spell while placing your grid as well. This way you will spend less time checking if it is safe to work on it and more time actually building up your energy in a safe place to work from. However, do not do this right when you start working. Choose a time that is long enough for you to finish your work, and take a break in between.

10) If you are familiar with your crystals already, then feel free to skip the below information - but if not, then please try to familiar yourself with them before attempting to work with them. For example, if you have never used crystal grids before then please try working on this page first before moving on...

1) There are five main different types of crystal that can be used in grids - quartz crystal points (Perfect), rose quartz crystals (Highly Recommended), moonstone crystals (Good), amethyst crystals (Poor), and black tourmaline stones (Bad). Below are a few websites that show a list of what each type of crystal is based on their look:

2) All crystals have a color, whether it be red, blue, yellow, green, or white. However, the colors should be chosen according to their energies - as this can prolong the life and effectiveness of your crystals greatly.

3) All crystals need to be cleansed before and after working with them. Crystal cleansing is a process whereby you remove the negative energy from the crystal and help to seal in their own natural energy so that they are 'recharged' and fully functional. Without cleansing your crystals, it is like trying to put something in a broken computer when all you have is an empty shell.

4) Hone Your Psychic Abilities – Crystals can be used as an essential component of psychic readings with both psychics and clients. Crystals can help facilitate clairvoyant readings, enhance the ability to receive information from a tarot reading or provide healing by helping in the process of channeling love, light or other life-force energies into another person.

5) Tap Into Your Spiritual Energy – Crystal grids can be used for spiritual cleansing, meditation, and to relax into the spiritual world. They can also help you to align your energy with the Earth's so as to draw in more of it and attune yourself more fully to nature.

6) Create A Safe Space – Crystal grids can be used as protection for a person or a place. They are especially effective for casting anti-black-magic spells, shielding people from energies that would harm them, or just creating a sacred space that is pure and free of negative energies.

7) Guard Your Privacy – Crystal grids are especially good at keeping unwanted people out of your private space. They can also be used to protect an area from spells that you may have to perform.

8) Enhance The Aura Behind Your Own Personal Protection Spell(s) – Crystals can be very helpful in creating a strong, powerful protective aura that will help to protect you from outside energy, and even strengthen and enhance the protection spell itself.

9) Create A Sacred Space – Crystal grids are also useful in creating a space that is sacred and filled with peace and love. This is especially helpful when dealing with self-love issues by allowing you to focus on healing within your own body first, before moving forward into deeper spiritual healing work.

10) Enhance Your Psychic Ability – Crystal grids are excellent in enhancing psychic abilities by opening up and activating the parts of the mind that are normally shut off. Crystals also increase the amount of psychic energy you have available to you, which can help to give you a greater range of abilities when working with other forms of energy.

11) Enhance The Psychic Abilities Of Your Clients — This is especially true when working with crystal grids. They can help you to connect with clients on an unconscious, spiritual level, helping them to heal much more easily and quickly. They can also help clients work through issues that they may be having by removing their mental blocks, and thus making it easier for them to progress in their own healing journey.

12) Use Crystal Grids To Enhance The Effectiveness Of Your Spells — Crystal grids can make your spells more effective by giving you a greater amount of energy that you can use for your spell. They can also help to align the energies of the universe with those of your spell, which will bring it into manifestation quickly and effectively.

13) Improve Your Psychic Abilities — One of the biggest reasons that people use crystal grids is because they want to improve their psychic abilities, or tap into powers that they do not have yet. With crystal grids, this is completely possible (and often very simple). They can help you to connect with the spirit world, make it easier for you to see the future and more clearly, and help you to receive information easily.

14) Increase Your Energy — When using crystal grids they can be very helpful in increasing your energy. This is especially true if you are working on a health issue (recovering from illness, injury or surgery), or if you have a lot of work to get done in a short period of time. Your psychic abilities will increase as well when your energy increases, as noted above.

15) Increase Your Knowledge — Crystal grids are excellent tools for increasing your knowledge. This can be especially true if you are trying to learn something new, or if you are just generally interested in many different aspects of life. Working with a crystal grid is an excellent way to speed up the process of learning as it will help to open up previously hidden information and truths that would otherwise be locked safely away from you.

16) Enhance Your Capacity For Spiritual Work – Crystals can be useful for enhancing your capacity for spiritual work, allowing you to connect more deeply with the inner self and the spiritual world without having to meditate for hours each day. You can do this while you are still awake and focusing on your spiritual work.

17) Improve Your Psychic Abilities – Crystals can be very useful in improving your psychic abilities, especially if you are working on the 5th chakra. They can help you to see even deeper into the next chakra, helping you to work from a pure place and direct your energies even more efficiently.

18) Enhance Your Psychic Abilities – Crystal grids can be used in three ways for spiritual purposes - by being a protective shield between you and the spirit world, by giving you access to a greater amount of energy that is already within you (so that it does not have to be drawn from outside sources), and thus allowing for greater psychic abilities.

19) Allow You To See Into The Future With Greater Accuracy – A crystal grid can be very effective in allowing you to see into the future with greater accuracy. This is especially true if you are using actual quartz crystal points, but it can also be effective with any type of quartz crystal.

20) Tap Into Your Natural Healing Abilities – If you are working with crystal grids to enhance your natural healing abilities, then they can be very effective in doing so. Their ability to increase energy levels and also to promote higher levels of psychic abilities can help you to tap into your own natural healing powers that much more easily.

21) Create A Protection Spell – Crystal grids can be very effective in creating protective shields and seals. This can be especially true when you are working on the 5th chakra and using large quartz crystal points, but even if you are working on the chakras above or below the 5th it will still work.

22) Create A Spiritual Healing Spell – Using crystal grids to create a spiritual healing spell is one of the best ways to benefit from them. In this case, you should use medium sized quartz crystal points for your grid, as they will give you a stronger effect and help to align the energies of your spell more efficiently than small or large ones would. You can then use your spells in a variety of ways from healing yourself to helping others.

23) Attune Yourself To Nature – Crystal grids can be very helpful in attuning you to nature. This is because they work by invoking the spirit of the Earth and by allowing it to do part of the work for you. You will have more energy available to you at all times, and your psychic abilities will naturally increase as a result.

24) Enhance Your Ability To Manifest Positive Things – By using crystal grids for manifesting positive things, you are tapping into the universal energies that are already at work within us all. This will help you to make more effective use of your own natural healing powers, and will also help you to create an environment for yourself that is conducive to healing.

25) Attune Yourself To Your Own Natural Potency – When using crystal grids, it is helpful to attune yourself not only to the Earth's energy but also your own natural potency. This allows you to use the energy more effectively and with greater precision.

26) Draw On The Power Of The Universe To Enhance Your Abilities – By drawing on the power of the universe using the energies of a crystal grid, you are tapping into a different level of universal energy than you would usually have access too. This will help you to work on more serious problems with ease and to help others in great need. This can be done by making a grid on paper, or working with actual crystals (either one or a combination of the two).

27) Become A Crystal Master – By using crystal grids, you are expanding and enhancing your own psychic abilities. This is because crystal grids are excellent tools for opening up the hidden energies that are locked within us all. When this happens, you will start to see how your crystals and the powers that they give you can be used in ways beyond what you previously imagined.

CONCLUSION

A lot of people think that crystals are just fancy jewelry. They believe that crystals aren't worth investing in because they lose their energy and won't be able to help them out in the long run. However, with a little bit of research and some crystal knowledge, you'll see that this isn't true at all. You'll also discover the many different benefits of using crystals in your life, such as:

Energizing your home or office space - one thing you might not know is that there are specific qualities to certain stones - meaning certain stones will have more positive effects on productivity than others.

Strengthening self-esteem - lots of people across the world use crystal therapy for this very reason. There are also lots of online communities where you can find more info about this.

Creating different life experiences - crystals are believed to align with certain astrological signs and meanings. This means that people who are born under the same sign can receive lots of help from crystals.

Making you happier - there are lots of ways that these stones can make you feel better emotionally – for example, if you're dealing with stress, you might try meditating with a crystal, like rose quartz or an amethyst. The stone will help to bring more positivity into your life, and create a better energy around your job or school.

Stronger immune system and healthier skin - lots of people who use crystals for healing and also using this stone as a regular part of their diet have seen incredible changes in their skin. The skin can feel more radiant and younger.

Opening your mind - there are many different types of crystals that you can use for this purpose - you might try smudging a sage bundle (which is used to cleanse the crown chakra) to open up your mind to new ideas.

Bringing good luck - if you wear or carry stones such as amethyst, tiger's eye, rose quartz or bloodstone, these stones are believed to bring the wearer good luck. If you suffer from bad luck, you might want to give it a try!

In addition to these helpful uses of crystal therapy, there are also crystals that can help with things like pain management and protecting your home from negative energy. If you want to learn about different types of crystals and how they can help you in your life, check out different books or online communities – most people who believe in the power of these stones are more than willing to talk about it and tell others about their experiences.

Here are some of the most popular crystals:

Amethyst – This stone is used for meditation and attuning to higher self. It brings peace and clarity. It is said to slow down a busy mind and make healing more palatable.

Crystal Quartz – This is one of the best all-purpose stones. It's said to be great for anything from purification to healing, cleansing, protection, removing negativity, attracting good luck or prosperity, or strengthening the aura. For more advanced work with quartz you can check out books on crystal healing.

Clear Quartz – One of the most well-known stones, clear quartz is a good stone to use for grounding and cleansing. When used in meditation it's believed to help in the development of psychic abilities. It also has protective properties, making it a great stone to keep around.

Smoky Quartz – This stone is used for clearing out negative energy and bringing more positive energy into one's life. It is also used as a guide or counselor during spiritual ascension, and is said to help people have strong convictions about their future lives.

Garnet – This stone is known for its ability to protect the heart and create passion. It is also a good grounding stone, which can help you to think more clearly during emotional times.

Lapis Lazuli – This stone is great for meditation, and can bring insight into one's life purpose. It is also thought to be a good luck stone.

Sodalite – This is a very high-vibration crystal that helps its owner find peace and ground themselves during difficult times.

Blue Lace Agate – This stone aids in communication with animals and nature spirits. It's also believed to help with creativity, imagination and original thinking.

Amethyst - "Purple Passion" - Amethyst is a purple variety of Quartz. It is one of the most powerful stones for healing, spirituality, protection and abundance.

Aventurine - "Stone of Opportunity" - Aventurine is thermally stable, like quartz, and thus makes a great substitute for it. Often used in jewelry because it is a pretty green-colored stone.

Emerald – "Stone of Success" - Emerald is a green variety of Beryl. It has been considered one of the most precious stones for thousands of years. Thought to bring success in all areas of life by inspiring imagination and creativity.

Rose Quartz – "Stone of Love" - Rose Quartz is a pink variety of Quartz. It is the stone of unconditional love. An extremely popular and widely used stone for healing, rose quartz also opens the heart to all types of love (not just romantic).

Tiger's Eye – "Stone of Focus" - Tiger's Eye is an orange/brown variety of Quartz. For millennia, Tiger's Eye has been used as a protective amulet against negative energy. Its properties include courage and strength, especially when faced with adversity or fear; it is thought to increase energy levels and stamina; and it promotes passion for life.

Crystals can be a lot of fun. They're also extremely useful in healing, protection, and overall well-being. Just remember that even though some crystals may have powers beyond what we can explain or measure, they are not meant to be used in place of traditional medicine. Crystals such as amethyst are often used while taking painkillers or prescription drugs to help with side effects and pain. Choose your crystals carefully and only use them when necessary, and always feel free to check with your doctor first.

Crystal is a powerful tool that can be used for energy work, accessing the Akashic Records, manifesting desires and intentions, and divination. It is also an excellent material to incorporate into ceremonies or rituals involving other stones. But this crystalline form of silicon dioxide isn't just for magicians or healers. Anyone can use crystals in their everyday life as they help align the body's chakras and promote consciousness expansion.

Crystal is a powerful tool for healing and self-improvement, bringing powerful energy into the body. It also releases negativity in the body. Crystal is used to heal and protect the body from disease and negative energy. It can also enhance our psychic abilities. Crystal can increase intuition, deep meditation, creativity and psychic awareness of thoughts and feelings. Crystal can be used to enhance dream recall by increasing lucidity of dreams. Crystal promotes physical growth, including healing of bones, muscles and tendons as well as promoting the health of all internal organs.

The dictionary definition of crystal is...

A clear or translucent mass in which no impurities are visible through optical or transmitted light; a gemstone composed solely (or mainly) of such a substance... A substance in which the atoms or molecules are arranged in a regular, unbroken, and three-dimensional pattern...

The dictionary definition of crystal is any clear or translucent mass that contains no impurities. This is not a good definition for this book, as the book focuses on healing crystals. The word gemstone is used to mean when any material that people consider to be precious, such as a diamond. This does not apply to this book. The actual definition of crystal is silicon dioxide or quartz (silicon dioxide would be considered an amorphous form of quartz).

Silica (SiO_2) occurs as cubic crystals which are identical to those formed by pressing together large plates of ordinary window glass (SiO_2).

Crystals are clear or translucent masses in which no impurities are visible through optical or transmitted light. Crystals have a regular, unbroken three-dimensional patterns. Crystals are composed of silicon dioxide (SiO_2), a chemical compound. Silicon is the second most abundant element in Earth's crust, occurring in its pure form as quartz and composed of either of two other polymorphic twins called cristobalite and tridymite. This definition is the one that will be used as it applies to healing crystals.

It is very rare for crystals to occur naturally as single entities, however, some transparent crystals can be found in this form.

Crystal healing has been used since around 200 B.C.

Around 200 B.C in Mesopotamia, the first writings about crystal healing were written by Sumerians. They used crystals in their rituals and used them to cure specific ailments. They also used crystals with amethyst and crystal quartz (silicon dioxide).

In antiquity, crystal healing was practiced via Feng Shui, a Chinese practice for balancing the environment of homes, business buildings, gardens, locations and land. It is believed that all things within the home are a reflection of its surroundings; therefore it is considered important to balance the energy of any space that we inhabit or work in with natural minerals found in each area. Feng Shui was used both to benefit the people who lived where the energy was balanced and to ward off misfortune.

In the ancient Greek world, crystal healing was given great importance. It formed part of their religion in the temples and was used in many of their rituals. Crystals were used for cleansing and purification by putting them into vases of water, making them holy or cleansing water. Crystals were well known because they sparkled under sunlight or moonlight and at night when any light shone on them, they shone more brightly than other crystals. Crystals were used as beacons, especially for travelers who saw their light and knew that they were travelling safely.

In the Middle Ages, crystal healing was part of alchemy. Crystals came up in many alchemical writings and were associated with healing; they were seen as having spiritual properties. In medieval times, people believed that crystals had the same four elements as we do - earth, air, fire and water - but that certain crystals had two of these elements whereas others only had one. These crystals are said to have existed from the dawn of time.

The Greeks, Egyptians, Sumerians and people from ancient times used crystals for healing. Crystals have been used in many other cultures throughout history, including Native American, Asian and African tribes. Records show that crystals were worn as amulets to ward off evil spirits and protect against ill-health.

Many feel a strong need for the earth element in their lives and find it difficult to achieve balance with the other three elements - fire, air and water.

Healing crystal is an essential component of many ancient systems of mysticism related to the mind-body relationship for healing purposes as well as those who heal on a spiritual level which have no particular religion attached to them or which are not tied down by doctrines or dogmas.

Many people who have used crystals to work with energy, have discovered that the energies are very strong. Many people who practice healing crystal have felt a connection with other people or higher powers.

Crystals have many qualities, which make them powerful tools for healing and spiritual growth. They have such power because they are associated with the earth and can help you attune to the earth's energies. This energy helps us to balance our bodies with our emotions, spirit and soul.

There are a large number of different crystals, which all contain positive energies; it is just a matter of finding your own personal power crystals or combination of crystals.

Crystals are often associated with other aspects of nature such as flowers, trees and herbs. There is no limit to the effect crystals can have on your life if you connect them with the earth and your spirit.

Crystal healing can help heal ailments in many ways, including spiritual, physical or mental. It can also bring about new spiritual awareness or a stronger spirituality. As well as healing you physically, crystals can help with healing your soul; this is what crystal healing is primarily about and it works in many different ways depending on its use.

In crystal healing it is believed that every person has a personal stone which will enhance their energy and bring them closer to their true selves. It is important to find your own stone, which will suit you the best.

Crystals are also believed to hold a person's energy. Many crystals are associated with an element and some people believe that a crystal takes on the energy of the element when placed in contact with it, making the person who is wearing the crystal or carrying it more in tune with that element. It is said to be like tuning up a musical instrument and allowing someone else to play your music.

There are many different types of crystals, which have been used for healing by thousands of people for centuries and continue their use today.

Zebra Quartz is such a crystal. It has been used as a stone of protection by many cultures, including Native American tribes, and the Egyptians.

It comes in colors, such as black, brown and white. Many people also wear zebra quartz to help enhance their psychic abilities.

Zebra quartz is believed to have positive healing energy which helps to protect the wearer from outside influences and internal negative energy that could potentially harm them or be detrimental to their health.

Zebra quartz is said to promote balance in your life by bringing harmony between yin and yang energies. This helps you become more aware of yourself and other people around you so that you can deal with problems effectively.

Zebra quartz can help you to increase your intuition and understanding of the people around you, making it easier for you to recognize when someone is lying to you. It will enhance your creativity as well.

It is also believed that zebra quartz can help you make better decisions intuitively, rather than basing them on logic.

This stone also has the power to increase vitality and stimulate energy, having a positive effect on your health, in particular your digestive system and nervous system. It can also boost stamina so that you have more energy during the day and are able to complete any tasks with ease.

This stone is said to be one of the best stones to wear if you are going to face a difficult task or challenge because it will give you a feeling of self-confidence. It will also protect against any outside influences that could make the situation worse and prevent you from achieving your goal.

Zebra quartz is also believed to help you reach your full potential and achieve all that you desire in life.

If you are pregnant, zebra quartz can help reduce morning sickness and relieve cramps and pains. It can also boost fertility so that it is easier for you to become pregnant, and increase the chances of having a baby boy if that's what you're hoping for.

If you're a stone lover, this is a stone you'll want to have near your bedside. Zebra quartz can help ease falls and accidents as well as strengthen your memory. It can also help with insomnia and despair, and is said to keep away negativity.

Zebra quartz brings in good luck to the wearer, but it also protects against debilitating bad luck spells such as those which may be cast during the new moon or at other times when we are vulnerable to psychic attack. It will also protect us from the negative energy of all those nasty people who are jealous of our good fortune.

If you want to accomplish a dream, zebra quartz will help you to achieve it. It will help you in your relationships with other people and also with the love of your life. This stone can be used for psychic healing purposes, either on yourself or on another person.

It is believed that zebra quartz can help clear away any negative energies which may be attached to your physical body and some people say that it even has healing properties which will help dissociate these energies from your physical being.

Zebra quartz is useful when you have been through trauma of any kind or if you have a past-life regression, as it will allow you to move on from that experience quickly and easily.

Printed in Great Britain
by Amazon